BOMBS AND BOMBINGS

ABOUT THE AUTHOR

Captain Thomas Graham Brodie, M.B.E., B. A., is a native Miamian. He is retired from the Metro Dade Police Department where he rose through promotional examinations from patrolman to Police Captain in 8 years. The author spent 24 years on the bomb squad which he helped establish. He was a bomb specialist and a criminalist and supervised the crime scene section.

Captain Brodie disposed of 37 bombs which had been delivered to their targets by bombers and disposed of over 4,000 other bombs and tons of explosives recovered from terrorists. He investigated approximately 350 explosions and bombings. Fifty percent of the perpetrators were convicted. *The Miami Herald* described Captain Brodie as "a genuine hero" and "the technical expertise of his bomb squad as almost legendary."

Captain Brodie was knighted by Queen Elizabeth for his role in protecting the British Empire in the Caribbean against bombers. The author also starred in a police training film, "Bombs I, II, and III" with Mickey Rooney.

In the early 1970s, as one of only 19 experienced police bomb disposal technicians, Captain Brodie served as a consultant in the establishment of the National Bomb Data Center. As a charter member of the International Association of Bomb Technicians and Investigators, he served on the advisory committee for 13 years.

The first edition of his book *Bombs and Bombings* was described as being twenty years ahead of its time.

BOMBS AND BOMBINGS

A Handbook to Detection, Disposal and Investigation for Police and Fire Departments

Second Edition

By

CAPTAIN THOMAS GRAHAM BRODIE, M.B.E., B.A.

Bomb Specialist, Criminalist and Crime Scene Technician
Metro Dade Police Department (Retired)
Miami, Florida

With a Foreword by

Albert W. Gleason

Detective—Bomb Section
New York City Police Department (Retired)
Explosives Officer
Bureau of Alcohol, Tobacco and Firearms (Retired)
Washington, D.C.

CHARLES C THOMAS • PUBLISHER
Springfield • Illinois • U.S.A.

Published and Distributed Throughout the World by

CHARLES C THOMAS • PUBLISHER
2600 South First Street
Springfield, Illinois 62794-9265

©*1996 by* CHARLES C THOMAS • PUBLISHER

ISBN 0-398-06551-9   (cloth)
ISBN 0-398-06552-7   (paper)

Library of Congress Catalog Card Number: 95-23030

With THOMAS BOOKS *careful attention is given to all details of manufacturing
and design. It is the Publisher's desire to present books that are satisfactory as to their
physical qualities and artistic possibilities and appropriate for their particular use.*
THOMAS BOOKS *will be true to those laws of quality that assure a good name
and good will.*

Printed in the United States of America
SC-R-3

Library of Congress Cataloging-in-Publication Data

Brodie, Thomas G.
    Bombs and bombings : a handbook to detection, disposal, and
investigation for police and fire departments / by Thomas Graham
Brodie ; with a foreword by Albert W. Gleason.—[2nd ed.]
        p.   cm.
    Includes index.
    ISBN 0-398-06551-9 (cloth). — ISBN 0-398-06552-7 (pbk.)
    1. Bombs.   2. Explosives.   3. Bomb reconnaisance.   I. Title.
TP270.B76   1995
623.4'51—dc20   95-23030
                                                                  CIP

TO MY FAMILY

FOREWORD

Prior to 1969 there were fewer than two dozen full-time police bomb technicians within the United States. In 1969 the number of bombings and bomb threats grew rapidly and a serious problem was getting worse. It was at this time that The International Association of Chiefs of Police assembled an Advisory Group of Bomb Technicians to outline methods and procedures necessary to combat the bomber. This group assisted in the preparation of and the presentation of training programs regarding bomb threats, explosive and incendiary device construction and identification, and bomb scene investigation. They were also involved in the formation and operation of a National Bomb Reporting System and the dissemination of technical information to police agencies nationwide. In addition, during this time, required bomb technician tools and equipment was recommended and in some instances designed and manufactured.

Tom Brodie was a member of this I.A.C.P. Bomb Advisory Group. For over thirty-five years he has been in the forefront in training, assistance to technicians and in combatting the bomber. He is a charter member of The International Association of Bomb Technicians and Investigators and served for several years on the Advisory Committee. He regularly attends chapter and regional meetings and is ever present at the International Conference. Although Tom is now retired from police work, he is still privately active and is always willing to assist anyone, anytime and in any way he can.

This is Tom's second edition on *Bombs and Bombings* and again he has followed his instincts and has given pride of place to his material and the beneficial applications that may be derived from it. Again, his writings emanate from real world experiences and he has dealt in greater detail than other writers have on the fundamental and practical aspects of his subject.

Tom has been a long-time friend and associate of mine. His dedication to the profession and his willingness to be of assistance are well known. It's Tom's hope that this book will aid in serving those dedicated professionals who bear the responsibility for the protection of life and property and the suppression of crimes involving the use of explosives.

ALBERT W. GLEASON

PREFACE

This book was written to answer the inquiries received from many sources concerning the subject of bombs and bombings. The author hopes that the information contained herein may help save lives and property. The book is not intended to make experts of readers or to assume any responsibility arising therefrom. The following pages contain a general outline of the procedures employed in processing commercial or homemade explosives, military explosive ordnance, suspected packages, infernal machines, bomb scares, explosions, bombings and similar incidents. Examples are given to explain the reasons for these procedures.

It is stressed at the outset that the construction of the bomb or the infernal machine and the conditions of the emergency situation will rarely be exactly the same. No single procedure can be utilized in each and every instance without deviation.

This written material relates to disposal and investigation of bombs, but it does not describe how to construct lethal devices. However, practical information on bomb evidence which is not found in other literature is in this volume.

Bomb and explosive disposal is a fascinating but hazardous field. Frivolous interest by poorly motivated persons is strenuously discouraged. Death or permanent injury can be the cost of poor judgment or inexperience. Books, courses and practice will not make a bomb expert, but these, accompanied by experience, will help a person become better at bomb disposal. Training and experience generate capability and good judgment. Excessive fear or overconfidence may cause the specialist to become his own worst enemy. While the experienced handler employing all of the accepted precautionary methods may minimize the risk of an untoward incident, it must be remembered that bombs and explosives are engineered, planned and ultimately designed to explode, and there is no absolutely safe method of handling many items.

It is possible to construct a bomb that cannot be deactivated. A bomb can be so sensitive to movement that it cannot be touched without its exploding.

New technology in the dismantling of bombs has increased the life expectancy of bomb disposal technicians. Yet many of those in bomb protection are not cognizant of their own essential needs: equipment, training, table of organization and procedures. The following pages do not describe how to solve all bomb problems, but they have been prepared as an approach to one of the most difficult of all police challenges and are intended to serve in an educational and constructive manner.

T.G.B.

ACKNOWLEDGMENTS

Most of the photographs are through the courtesy of the Metro Dade Police Department.

Drawings were prepared by Lieutenant Paul Janofsky and Faith Brodie Wheeler. Al Gleason, Major Ralph Way, U.S.M.C., Red Moody and Gerd Ester were contributors.

I wish to thank all those with whom I have ever worked.

CONTENTS

BOMBS AND BOMBINGS

Chapter 1

EXPLOSIVE AND BOMB DISPOSAL
SERVICES AND TRAINING

Obtaining adequate equipment for competent bomb handling is usually a difficult process. The best method is to educate those persons in charge of the department. This can include using all available data on bomb scares, stolen and recovered explosives, and actual bombs and bombings. Although state and local incidents should be stressed, importance should be given to national and international incidents as well as to military and commercial explosive usage. Surveys of possible local government and industry vulnerability also help show needs that should be met. Sometimes past experience demonstrates a need for bomb protection equipment and the organization of operating procedures. Dade County, Florida, acquired training and equipment for its bomb squad in the early sixties after a series of right-wing bombings, labor bombings and increased seizures of bomb caches of revolutionaries in the greater Miami area. Figures 2 and 3 were outstanding examples. Everyone who recognizes a need for adequate equipment and training should not hesitate to bring it to the attention of responsible people.

Too often, police and fire agencies wait until a bomb is found or a tragedy occurs before a decision is made to take precautionary measures for the future. Even though a department may have trained personnel, equipment and tactical plans for such an emergency, an officer who is not a bomb specialist will sometimes handle a bomb himself before he calls for skilled assistance.

TACTICAL PLANS

Every police and fire department should have a tactical plan prepared for use in the event of an explosion or a bomb incident. Who is going to dispose of a bomb? It is the responsibility of the police or fire administrator to have his personnel know whom to call to the scene. The more experience the bomb specialist has, the safer he is. Frequently an officer

3

Figure 1. The author is shown instructing a group of visiting police officials from the Philippines. Knowledge and motivation are two of the basic principles of bomb protection.

who has had very little training and possesses very little equipment assumes, or is given, the responsibility of bomb disposal. However, it is necessary to determine who the best specialist is and where and how he can be obtained. One man cannot be completely depended upon, since he may be out of the vicinity at the time. One or more backup specialists are also necessary.

The number of explosive and bomb cases and related duties may justify a full-time bomb squad like the Metro Dade County Police have as shown in Figure 4. Since joining a bomb squad requires a major change in job duties, before a person becomes a bomb disposal technician (also called a bomb technician, bomb specialist or bomb tech) and is sent to the Hazardous Devices School, he should be forewarned of all problems of becoming a bomb disposal technician. These problems are:

Figure 2. A series of labor bombings helped provide impetus for the development of the Dade County Bomb Squad. The investigation of this fatal bombing is being reopened because of connecting signature methods of the bombings.

Figure 3. This seizure of explosives and arms from a Miami Beach motel were destined for Fidel Castro, whose picture is in the center of the figure. The author disposed of over 4,000 bombs recovered from these terrorist groups.

Figure 4. The Dade County Bomb Squad is one of the most experienced bomb squads in the United States. Finances for personnel, training and equipment are directly related to their experience.

1. There is a greater danger of being killed, injured or disabled. The most common injuries are: loss of fingers, hands, eyesight and hearing. Victims of bomb injuries often have circulatory, respiratory, digestive and neurological problems. Bomb disposal technicians may be exposed to carcinogenic and other hazardous chemicals that may cause long-term illnesses.
2. There is a lack of adequate permanent medical, financial and psychological benefits for disabled officers and their families.
3. Anxiety develops for the bomb disposal technician, his family, friends and associates.
4. Being on call during off-duty hours is a nuisance, especially since there seldom is monetary compensation for the inconvenience.
5. The bomb technician risks possible loss of promotional eligibility due to being a specialist.
6. Bomb disposal technicians, their relatives or associates may be targets of terrorists and may be injured or killed by error, neglect, or as an intentional target of bombers.

7. Bomb disposal requires dirty, hard manual labor and long hours.

The above considerations may be used in requests for additional funds for equipment, training, hazardous-duty pay, tactical plans and a favorable table of organization.

A small police department may experience one bomb incident and then obtain elaborate equipment to deal with possible new incidents, when the actual chances for future needs are minimal. Such a department may be better off if they consider nearby outside assistance. A small department may decide to have their own equipment and personnel because they want to enhance their image; because they have poor rapport for one reason or another with a better-equipped, nearby agency; or because they have a sincere belief that time is the most important factor and that a risk should be taken in order "to do something themselves," even if it is the wrong thing.

The importance of thorough training for personnel assigned to bomb disposal work and of first-class equipment cannot be overemphasized. If the required time and money for the safety of personnel cannot be provided, then the administrator of the department may be responsible for his negligence in causing unnecessary risk of life and injury to his men. A superior officer who lacks disposal knowledge should not order a subordinate to dispose of an explosive item without full consideration of a specialist's opinion.

One of the biggest problems within a department is caused by men who are not assigned to the bomb squad but who have been in the armed forces or have limited experience in blasting. These men frequently handle bombs or explosives unnecessarily because they do not want to inconvenience the bomb squad. Departmental regulations should strictly prohibit this. The same type of attitude is found in civilians whose curiosity is aroused and who believe that "I was in the service and know all about explosives." Every large department will have case histories of explosive deaths and injuries caused by curiosity and ignorant boldness as shown in Figure 5.

AVAILABLE ASSISTANCE

Help from the Army explosive ordnance personnel (EOD) can be requested from anywhere in the United States by telephoning the United States Armed Forces Command (FORSCOM) EOD at (404) 363-5225.

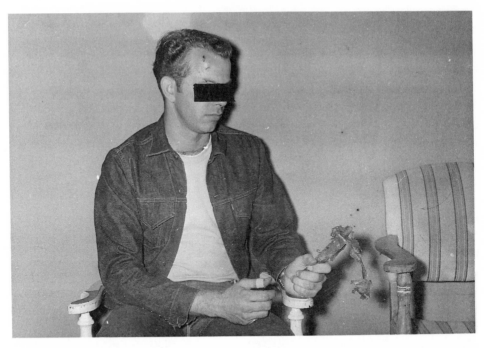

Figure 5. A Dade County citizen found a white phosphorus rifle grenade in a World War II ammo dump, broke it open, burned phosphorus and broke open the burster tube which burst on him, cutting his thumb and forehead.

They are located at Fort Gillem, Forest Park, Georgia 30050-5000. They are available twenty-four hours every day all year, including holidays. They may dispatch the closest Army Explosive Ordnance Disposal Detachment to the scene of an incident.

In addition, other EOD personnel of the local Air Force and Navy bases may volunteer their assistance. This assistance may depend on the policy of the EOD detachment or their base commanders.

There are limitations and problems in obtaining rapid assistance by the Armed Services. These are as follows:

1. The time involved in obtaining permission from the commanding officer and in traveling from the nearest base.
2. Posse comitatus, in which the Armed Forces cannot be used for public functions, i.e. searching for bombs or searching for evidence.
3. EOD personnel may render safe improvised explosive devices but are not allowed to accept, transport, store or dispose of commercial explosives or be involved in the chain of evidence in most situations. Exceptions to the above restrictions may be obtained only from FORSCOM.

4. Inexperience with bomb-scene investigation, evidence and court testimony. Military personnel may be unfamiliar with local laws and police procedures which may create problems when the case comes to trial.

SOURCES OF TRAINING

Training in explosives is available from somewhat limited sources. The Institute of the Makers of Explosives, Suite 310, 1120 Nineteenth Street, N.W., Washington, D.C. 20036-3602, may help for a small fee. They also provide dummy display only to police and fire personnel through the Federal Bureau of Investigation's National Bomb Data Center.

Explosive ordnance reconnaissance and disposal is taught without charge to police and fire personnel upon request to the United States FORSCOM in Fort Gillem, Forest Park, Georgia. The classes include both recognition of military ordnance and disposal of homemade bombs. These classes may last up to forty hours and may be given at any local police or fire station.

In order for a member of a state or local police or fire department to attend the Hazardous Devices School at Redstone Arsenal, Alabama and train to be a bomb disposal technician, the department must follow several guidelines. The student must be in good health, be able to perform certain physical tasks and be an asset to his or her community in bomb and explosive matters. The department must have these pieces of equipment: a complete bomb suit, a portable x-ray machine, a disrupter, a demolition kit and a set of dismantling tools. The basic four-week course and the one-week refresher course are free. Application is made only through the Federal Bureau of Investigation.

Foreign police, fire and military bomb disposal technicians are taught at a school in Louisiana under a contract with the United States State Department.

The Bureau of Alcohol, Tobacco and Firearms conducts a bombing investigation school for police and fire personnel at the Federal Law Enforcement Training Center at Glynco, Georgia.

The International Association of Bomb Technicians and Investigators conducts international, regional and chapter training conferences for police, fire and security personnel. Figure 6 shows an IABTI chapter

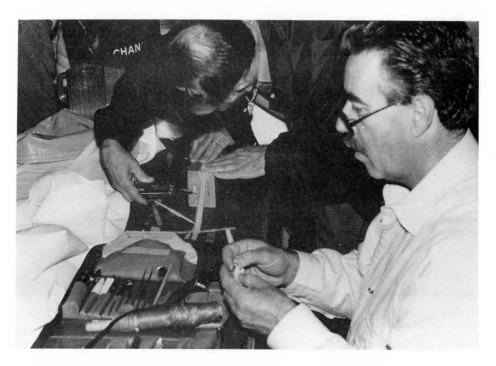

Figure 6. A hands-on training conference of the International Association of Bomb Technicians and Investigators where members learn and practice bomb disposal techniques. The author is a charter member of the IABTI and has never missed a chapter, regional or international meeting.

training conference. The association also produces a magazine and video training tapes.

Bruce Koffeler of Securesearch, Inc. provides training tapes, literature and dummy explosive and bomb display items.

LITERATURE

Literature in bomb disposal is limited. However, information is available in the following sources.

1. *Bombs, Explosives and Incendiary Devices,* by Richard A. Durfee, published by Police Science Press, Post Office Box 1468, Cocoa Beach, Florida (1961).
2. *Explosives and Homemade Bombs,* by Major Joseph F. Stoffel, published by Charles C Thomas, Springfield, Illinois (1972).

3. *Explosives and Bomb Disposal Guide,* by Robert R. Lenz, published by Charles C Thomas, Springfield, Illinois (1965).
4. *Explosives and Rock Blasting* prepared by The Atlas Powder Company, a Division of ICI Explosives, Dallas, Texas.
5. The National Bomb Data Center has published bulletins and manuals since its establishment in 1970. The NBDC is now at the Federal Bureau of Investigation.
6. *Bombers and Firesetters* by John MacDonald, published by Charles C Thomas, Springfield, Illinois.
7. *Protection Against Bombs and Incendiaries,* by Earl A. Pike, published by Charles C Thomas, Springfield, Illinois.

ORGANIZATION

Bomb squads have to establish a proper table of organization to insure safety in the accomplishment of their purpose of bomb disposal. All of the members of a bomb squad should be a close-knit team who are able to communicate easily with each other about training, equipment and intelligence information concerning the latest explosives and bombs in their jurisdiction, within their agency and worldwide. New York City established the first full-time (police) bomb squad in 1940 due to a major increase in bomb-related incidents.

For a department smaller than New York, which does not have as many bomb calls, there may not be enough business to keep one man occupied completely on bomb disposal work. The members of a bomb squad should all be in the same unit with similar assignments instead of being spread out in different sections of the department with dissimilar secondary duties. A one-man bomb squad is not adequate, since the man may be out of town on vacation or at school. Two men are better, but if one is out of town the other will have to be tied down both on duty and off duty. Three or four men make a good-size bomb squad for almost any department, as one of them can always be on call and available.

Most bombings occur at nights, during weekends or during irregular, unexpected times. Consequently, bomb disposal technicians are subject to being on on-call status and working overtime. For safety and coordination of work, all members of a bomb squad should have the same supervisor. Good lines of authority and responsibility are imperative for safety in bomb disposal work, even in the smallest bomb squads. If the bomb disposal technicians have secondary duties, they should still be coordinated under the same immediate supervisor.

Secondary duties should be closely allied as possible to bomb disposal work. The main secondary duty of most bomb disposal technicians is bomb scene or post-blast scene investigation. Some departments also use the bomb squad to examine arson scenes. Other allied secondary duties that may be assigned to the bomb squad include commercial explosive storage magazines and blasting procedures for safety practices and for the prevention of theft of explosives. Hazardous waste material duties are now often assigned to the fire department or dealt with by private contractors.

Bomb disposal technicians may also assist an investigation by tracing sources of bomb-making materials, laboratory examination of evidence, reconstruction of bombs, interview of suspects, storage of explosive evidence, explosive testing or rapid-entry assistance for hostage rescue. Bomb disposal technicians may also be trained as divers for underwater bomb cases.

Some departments utilize bomb disposal technicians for complete investigations of any explosive or arson-related crimes or for intelligence investigation, i.e. surveillance of suspects and undercover operations. Inherent problems of exposure to news media and emergency response time may create conflict for personnel to serve in both of these capacities as both bomb disposal technicians and investigators.

The particular division of government where bomb squads are assigned may relate to their secondary duties, if any, or for the convenience of management and budgeting. The primary concern of the bomb squad is for the accomplishment of bomb disposal in a safe manner.

Chapter 2

BOMB CARRIERS

PURPOSE OF A CARRIER

The purpose of a bomb carrier is to transport a bomb safely from the location where it was found to a location where it can be stored, deactivated, dismantled or blown. Dismantling an open or partly open bomb is usually simple, but a closed bomb may be considered too risky. There are many cases in which law enforcement personnel were killed dismantling bombs, because they did not have a bomb carrier or a disrupter. (Only an inexperienced person would believe that all bombs can be deactivated by hand.) A bomb carrier or a disrupter are not cure-alls, but they do eliminate much of the risk to a novice bomb disposal technician. Before disrupters were developed, the most simple approach for a novice bomb disposal technician was to utilize a remote-control device to set a bomb in a carrier as shown in Figure 7. Many factors could complicate this procedure, but it was the best known method for inexperienced technicians. Disrupters and dismantling methods are covered in the chapter on homemade bombs or improvised explosive devices (IED).

KINDS OF CARRIERS

The first known bomb carrier or container was developed by the Milwaukee, Wisconsin Police Department, after a bomb exploded in police headquarters. There are no records of any test of this vehicle, shown in Figures 8 and 9.

LaGuardia Pike Interwoven Steel Cable

There are five basic types of bomb carriers or containers which have been developed. As a result of two bomb squad men being killed in 1940 while dismantling a bomb, the New York City Police developed the first

Figure 7. The world's first top-vent bomb carrier which was developed by the author in 1961. Once a suspect bomb had been moved remotely, it could be placed into the container for transportation to a safe disposal area. Thousands of copies have been made since that time.

tested carrier. The LaGuardia Pike bomb truck is named after the mayor who provided the funding and Lieutenant Pike of the squad who did the testing. The container is made of interwoven 5/8-inch plow steel cable.

There are two layers of cable six inches apart and ten inches total thickness. The inside diameter is ten feet long, six feet wide and six feet high. The bomb is suspended in the center of this container. Most of the blast effect and shrapnel are stopped by the cable. Centering the explosive is important for the most effective attenuation (diminishing) of the explosive effects. Severe explosions which are near the limit of capability of the carrier cause blast to escape between the cables. If a person were standing adjacent to the carrier, he might be injured but not severely. New York City had two of these bomb trailers attached to semi-trailer trucks. The original cost in 1942 was $15,000 each. The only copy of this design was the United States Secret Service truck built in approximately 1946. The carrier was designed in the shape of a football and had only one layer of cable and smaller dimensions than the New York model. A slanted steel deflection plate on each side of the container deflected the

Figure 8. These officers are utilizing two principles of bomb protection: distance and barrier to remotely move a suspect practice bomb. This photograph of the Milwaukee Police Department bomb squad was taken in 1940.

Figure 9. This photograph was taken in Milwaukee in 1940 and shows that the safest method of bomb disposal is remote and is the prime consideration in every situation. Courtesy of former assistant Police Chief Raymond Dahl.

blast from the sides upward. This vehicle was not tested until approximately 1962, but the tests were not properly performed, so it was not too successful.

The New York City Containers were retested in the middle sixties by Detective Al Gleason and similar results to the first tests were found. A particular type of carrier or container should not be used unless its limitations are known.

In January, 1961, the author completed successful explosive tests for the first top-vented bomb carrier. The concept was an idea of Charles W. Zmuda, Chief of Central Services for the Metro Dade Police Department in Miami, Florida. The author wrote an article describing the tests and the vehicle with its equipment for the September, 1962 issue of *Police Chief* magazine. This was the first top-vented bomb container in the world. Thousands of copies have been made since that time.

A series of tests were conducted on various containers in an attempt to contain the explosion effects on the sides and bottom and direct the force upward. At this time, other police departments, steel companies, explosive companies and the armed forces were contacted for advice. It appeared that no one had ever explored the idea before. A series of safes and sand and air boxes were blown up in an effort to find what type of container was most effective.

Public safety departments have used other types of containers without proper testing. The effects of an explosion on some of these containers can be quite surprising. In our tests, our early prototype containers were completely destroyed. The explosion's effect is a rapid process of tremendous pressure being exerted in less than one second. If the container does not hold, it will be broken into fragments, which only add to the dangerous effects of the explosion. In brief, an explosion goes the path of least resistance, but it does not take the time to look for it.

Bob Dykes of the R.J. Dykes Iron Company provided information that the container must be round because square corners are weak points. Mr. Dykes also advised allowing ample spacing from the walls of the cylinder, centering a suspect bomb on dry and shock-absorbing sand at the bottom of the container. He further advised that the walls of the cylinder must be high enough to direct the force straight out the top. Dykes volunteered the use of a boiler. The first bomb carrier of the Metro Dade Police (formerly named the Dade County Public Safety Department) was built on these boiler specifications because this was the size of the container that was successfully tested. The proof is illustrated in Figures 10 and 11. The final product weighs 1,500 pounds and is 3½ feet in diameter and 4½ feet high. The side of the cylinder is made of ¾-inch thick cold-rolled steel, and the bottom is a ¾-inch spun-steel rounded boiler head as shown in detail in Figure 12.

Figure 10. The author used these 24 sticks of dynamite to prove that a top-vent carrier on a truck can successfully direct the explosion straight up into the air without injury to the driver or surrounding people or property.

Our final test was with 12 pounds (24-sticks) of 1¼ in. × 8 in. 40 percent nitroglycerine dynamite in a container that was only ⅜-inch steel. We never tested our ¾-inch thick container, since a large blast may weaken it (see Fig. 13).

Doctor Coy Glass of Aberdeen Proving Grounds advised that a minute hairline fracture may develop in a test explosion which may not even be seen in magnaflux x-raying of the steel. In the next blast, the pressure may get into the crack and rupture the container. Some containers have undergone over a hundred large demonstration explosions before failure.

The first police department to copy the top-vent container was Detroit, followed by Toronto, Nassau County and Puerto Rico. In 1972, the author worked with the National Bomb Data Center and the Battelle Research Center testing a six-foot diameter container which vented the explosion of fifty pounds of dynamite. The author further assisted many different agencies and companies in the development of vented cylindrical containers. Many of these are used as concealed containers near buildings or other possible bomb targets for placement of suspected bombs as shown in Figure 14.

Figure 11. This photograph proves that this relatively inexpensive truck has the same capacity as the more expensive interwoven steel cable truck. The twelve pounds of explosive or suspect bomb must be low enough in the container to make sure the main force of the explosion is directed straight up.

To safely use the top-vented carrier or container, the suspect bomb should be centered horizontally in a net on dry sand or vermiculite at the bottom of the container. The bomb should not be confined except for the possible use of a bomb blanket over the top of the carrier to catch fragmentation. If a bomb explodes too high in the container instead of being on the insulated bottom, the pressure of the explosion will not be directed upward but will spread outward over the top, possibly causing injuries or damage. The net is necessary to retrieve suspect bombs remotely from the container.

Bottomless Container

Around 1965, Los Angeles built a bomb container consisting of a vertical cylinder made of 1-in. cold-rolled steel, 3½ feet in diameter, and 4½ feet high. This container is mounted on a four-wheel trailer and has no bottom or top. The bomb is suspended on a canvas sling. Other departments copied this container without testing it first. Once tests were conducted, it was found that the explosion pressure from the bottom of

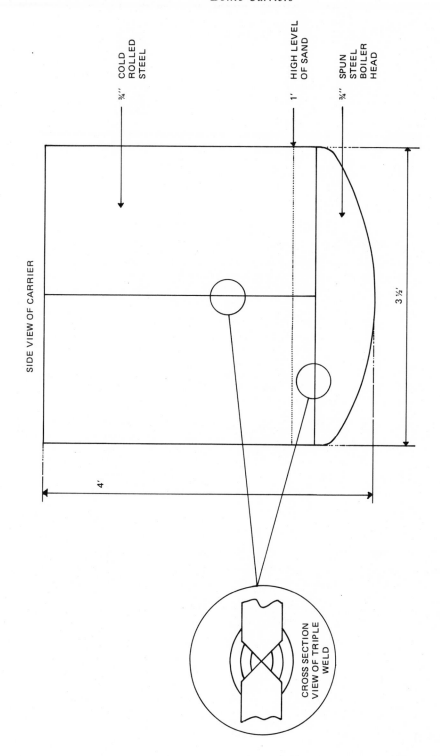

SIDE VIEW OF CARRIER

¾" COLD ROLLED STEEL

1' HIGH LEVEL OF SAND

¾" SPUN STEEL BOILER HEAD

3 ½'

4'

CROSS SECTION VIEW OF TRIPLE WELD

Figure 12. The welds of the container are done in layers in order to prevent weakening the steel.

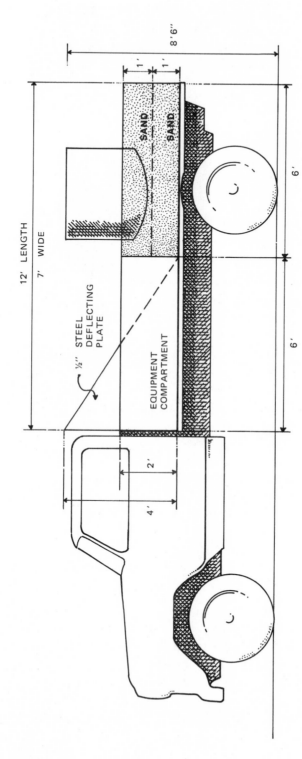

Figure 13. The container should be centered properly and be supported sufficiently with extra heavy-duty springs and dry sand or vermiculite.

Figure 14. The author assisted the United States Secret Service by testing this container before it was planted in the ground at Homestead Air Force Base where President Nixon used to land and depart on trips to his home in Miami. A manhole cover, flush with the ground, covers many of these containers for low-profile use.

the carrier is deflected from the ground and meets pressure from the top of the carrier. This reinforced pressure on the outside of the carrier can create unexpected injuries and damage. It is best to use only a type of container that has been tested.

Sand Truck Carrier

Dump trucks may be used in an emergency to transport suspected bombs. The size of the bomb is determined by the size and weight of the truck carrying it. A shallow indentation dug into the top of the sand will accommodate small bombs. If the indentation is too shallow, the explosion will not be deflected upwards. If the indentation is too deep, then an explosion may destroy the truck. Again, before the need arises, test a sand truck to determine if it would suit your purposes.

Jordan Complete Confinement Container

The concept of a complete confinement container was the result of the persistence and innovation of Rod Jordan, an engineer of Picatinny Arsenal whose job was to research and develop Army Explosive Ordnance Disposal tools. After the first meeting of the National Bomb Data Center in 1970, Mr. Jordan had the containers built following records of attempts to destroy an unused test container for the first atomic bomb.

There are two types of complete confinement containers. The horizontal cylinder has tremendous inside capacity and allows the entire entrance of small robots. The spherical container, as shown in Figure 15, is less expensive and comes in two sizes. There is very little motion when a bomb explodes in the middle of the container. This is not really a complete confinement because the pressure escapes from the container through a small hole over a long period of time. The container whistles like a tea kettle after the explosion. The capacity of a six-foot sphere has been estimated to be as high as eighty pounds of C4 plastic explosive.

The disadvantage of using the spherical complete confinement container is that heat is trapped with the bomb fragments for a long time, causing any evidence that is not destroyed by the pressure to be burned to a crisp. Other disadvantages are the high price in comparison to other containers, the small opening for introduction of the suspect bomb, and the doorway must be closed and secured after the bomb is centered in the container.

New York and the Secret Service replaced their interwoven steel containers with spheres. The spherical containers are much smaller yet will safely confine a larger explosive force than the old cable containers. Spherical containers can be used low profile in camouflaged vehicles. Hydraulic, portable, radio-controlled handtrucks can even carry the

Figure 15. The author is admiring a complete confinement container on a self-propelled cart that can be used on freight elevators. These spheres are sold separately or may even be remotely controlled.

container inside buildings on elevators. This is exceptional equipment and is a big step forward in bomb protection. Bomb technicians owe a debt of gratitude to Rod Jordan and other researchers.

VEHICLE

Both a truck and a trailer to carry the bomb container have their advantages and disadvantages. On our test with 12 pounds of dynamite on a truck, none of the glass or springs were broken and none of the tires were blown out. Cardboard boxes on sticks around the truck were not moved. A stick under the body of the truck was driven down only about three inches into soft sand. The type of vehicle that is chosen to transport a bomb carrier should be tested. The author privately assisted in the explosive tests of a top-vented container on a trailer for the Criminalistics Company as shown in Figure 16. Heavy springs, axles, hitch, brakes and towing ease are all major considerations in a proven vehicle.

Many decisions must be made in the selection of the type of truck or

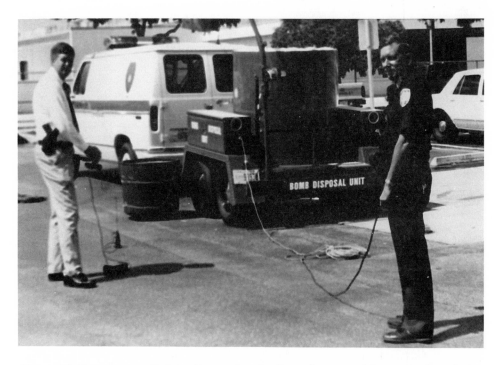

Figure 16. Remote-controlled loading and unloading of suspected improvised explosive devices or sensitive explosives helps to alleviate the risk in bomb disposal. Command may be wire or radio control from long distances.

trailer. Multi-purpose vehicles may be easier to obtain for budgetary concerns. Purpose of the vehicle, safety, terrain, traffic congestion, ease of use, number of operators and size of the area to be covered are some of the factors that determine one's choice of carriers. Besides bomb disposal, the vehicle may have to be used for patrol, investigation, explosive recovery, hazardous waste disposal, bombing scene investigation or under-water recovery. It should be decided whether all of this additional equipment will be carried on a truck, a trailer or a towing vehicle. After receiving a call, time should not be spent loading equipment onto an emergency vehicle.

USE OF THE CARRIER

Whenever a bomb call is received, the bomb carrier should be taken along, because although the complainant may advise that he has a blasting cap, when you arrive you may find that the item is a bomb. The converse may also be true: the complainant may advise he has a bomb, but he may have only a blasting cap. If you arrive at the scene without a bomb carrier and your equipment, you may be placed in the embarrassing position of having to take some action immediately but without proper equipment. That is not the time to wish you had taken the bomb vehicle with you.

Chapter 3

EQUIPMENT

MINIMUM EQUIPMENT NEEDED

There are variations in the kinds of tools preferred by bomb technicians. The equipment is described at the beginning of the book so that you will not have to look back to an appendix to see what it is that the text is explaining. Years ago, the most common tools used by bomb technicians were a line, a knife and a wire cutter. Now the most common tool is the disrupter.

The Hazardous Devices School requires that a student's department must have a disrupter, a bomb suit, a portable x-ray machine and a demolition kit as prerequisites to attendance.

The following pieces of equipment, used by the Metro Dade Police Department, have all been found useful through the years. Some equipment has been obtained and used in practice but was never found to be of use in actual cases of recovered explosives, bombs and bombings. Discussion of the use and relative importance of this equipment will be found in Chapter 7 on improvised explosive devices.

BOMB DISPOSAL EQUIPMENT

1. Truck or trailer with bomb container. Equipment may be carried on a trailer or towing vehicle with emergency lights, siren, two-way radio and public address speaker. The truck or trailer should have the capability of transporting a robot which is always kept in readiness on the vehicle.
2. The disrupter is the most essential and the most commonly used piece of bomb disposal equipment today. Figure 17 illustrates a widely used disrupter with the latest state-of-the-art development.
3. A robot or means of delivering a disrupter remotely. The robots shown in Figures 18, 19 and 20 are the most commonly used robots proven to be effective throughout the world. New, smaller robots are being developed as shown in Figure 21. The shield or sled in

26

Figure 17. Disrupters may be improvised from a piece of pipe and end cap for less than a dollar or they can be carefully manufactured into precise and proven equipment as shown.

Figure 22 can be improvised for less than $2,000. Remote arms are illustrated in Figure 23.

4. CO_2 fire extinguisher.
5. Dry chemical extinguisher.
6. First-aid kit with large supply of burn ointment.
7. Area map, report and receipt form.
8. Remote moving and door opening tools.
9. Two complete bomb suits and helmets with ventilation and built-in two-way communications.
10. Fire blanket.
11. Two pairs of steel mesh gloves.
12. Demolition kit:
    a. Fuse detonators.
    b. Electric detonators.
    c. Squibs.
    d. Safety fuse.
    e. Fuse lighters.

Figure 18. The British Wheelbarrow was the first bomb disposal robot. Research and development was financed by the British government to deal with improvised explosive devices in Ulster. This robot has been used many times and has saved many lives.

Figure 19. The Canadian government supplemented expenses in the development of their robots. The manufacturer produced a popular piece of equipment which has greatly helped bomb disposal technicians.

      f. Cap crimper.
      g. Galvanometer.
      h. Blasting machine.
      i. Radio-controlled initiator and receivers.

Figure 20. Every bomb squad should have a robot. The manufacturer of the equipment shown provides a wide variety of remote equipment and has done so at the advice of his customers.

13. Explosives:
    a. Plastic explosive.
    b. Detonating cord.
    c. Electric blasting wire.
    d. Electrical tape.
14. Portable x-ray machine, fluoroscope screen, extension cord and lead shielding.
15. Radiation film badges indicating x-ray exposure.
16. Polaroid film developer.
17. Military ordnance, chemical and explosive manuals.
18. Tool box of dismantling tools:
    a. Fiber optic lights.
    b. Probes.
    c. Knives.
    d. Wire cutters.
    e. Pliers.
    f. Needle-nose pliers.
    g. Pipe wrenches.
    h. Hammers.
    i. Chisels.
    j. Adjustable wrenches.
    k. Screwdrivers.

Figure 21. This inexpensive robot has a wide variety of uses. Different configurations permit the machine to travel in small confined areas.

     l. Crowbar.

    m. Pipe vise.

     n. Hacksaws.

     o. Bolt cutter.

     p. Shape charge containers.

     q. Glass knives.

     r. Tweezers.

     s. Scalpels.

     t. Clamps.

19. Shovel and axe.
20. Heavy fishing string and ropes.
21. Radiological survey meters and protective clothing.
22. Three explosive storage magazines are a necessity for storage of bulk explosive evidence, detonators and fireworks. None of the three above items should ever be kept together.
23. A bomb disposal or blasting range with a block house for viewing and photography of controlled explosions.

Figure 22. The shield or sled can be used to safely dismantle or move a bomb at a distance of eight feet. This is a poor man's robot but is better than a bomb suit because it provides distance.

BOMB DETECTION AND BOMB SEARCH EQUIPMENT

The pieces of equipment listed above have all been used. Equipment listed below may be used in bomb disposal work but are multiple purpose. They are most commonly used to detect bombs, to prevent the intrusion of bombs into an area, or to search for bombs that may be present in the area.

1. A dog is shown in Figure 24 and/or an electronic explosive vapor detector depicted in Figure 25.
2. Listening device.
3. Metal detectors may be a hand-held wand, a minesweeper or a stationary portal to search persons or objects like mail. (Magnetometers only detect iron or steel. Metal detector is the correct term for a more effective detector than a magnetometer.)
4. Large x-ray machines for searching luggage and parcels for bombs as well as other weapons.

Figure 23. Remote handling or dismantling arms can be used with protective clothing or from behind a shield.

EXPENDABLE ITEMS

1. Two pairs of ice tongs with extra teeth now are rarely used due to the development of disrupters.
2. A tank of liquid nitrogen with a valve and a needle nozzle with a styrofoam icebox was used experimentally by the Metro Dade Police but was never found to be useful on suspected improvised explosive devices.
3. Shotguns and rifles with modified grenade launchers were found useful but were replaced by disrupters.

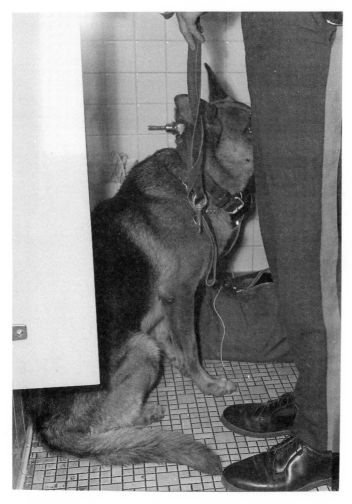

Figure 24. This explosive detection dog has alerted on an abandoned satchel in a rest room at the Miami International Airport. The dog sits down in a passive signal. The bag contained shoe polish which is nitrobenzene.

Figure 25. Man-made explosive detectors are best used in routine search of visitors, vehicles and containers for extensive time periods. This detector is very sensitive, gives instant readings and clears itself quickly.

Chapter 4

DEFINITIONS AND CHARACTERISTICS
OF EXPLOSIVES

TYPES OF EXPLOSIONS

There are five types of explosions: (a) steam as exemplified in Figure 26 or mechanical as shown in Figure 27, (b) chemical, (c) atomic, (d) nuclear, and (e) electrical. One definition of an explosion is a bursting outward or a sudden movement from one place to another. An implosion is a bursting inward, as in the collapse of a vacuum, i.e. a television tube breaking or the implosion after an explosion as seen in Figure 28.

Figure 26. Shown are the effects from a steam explosion. A gasoline-saturated rug burning hotly on terrazzo or cement turns moisture in the cement to steam, making irregular craters. Novice investigators often mistake these craters for chemical explosion craters.

A mechanical explosion can be defined as a sudden and violent release of pressure initiated by its own pressure and/or heat or a combi-

35

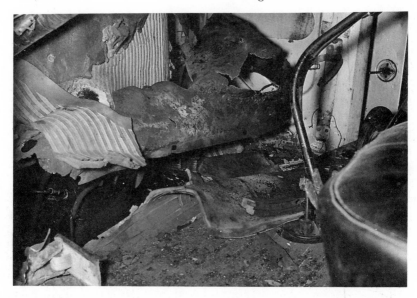

Figure 27. Mechanical explosion of a flywheel in a diesel truck. This happens occasionally also in drag racers. The absence of explosive residue and heat are just two of the indicators that it was not a bomb.

nation of extraneous heat or pressure. An atomic explosion is the sudden release of tremendous amounts of heat, gaseous pressure and radiation as a result of splitting the nuclei of a heavy atom into lighter atoms. A nuclear explosion is the sudden release of tremendous amounts of radiation as a result of fusing the nuclei of light atoms. Doctor Joseph Davis, the medical examiner of Dade County, Florida, states that an electrical explosion is a phenomena that occurs by the rapid exchange or vaporization of material that occurs in electrocutions.

PARTS OF AN EXPLOSIVE

A chemical explosive is an unstable compound or mixture which, upon initiation, undergoes a rapid exchange of ions, resulting in large amounts of heat and gaseous pressure, usually accompanied by a loud report. An explosive can be a solid, liquid or gas.

Pyrolysis is the chemical decomposition of a substance through the action of heat. When wood is heated it forms a vapor with air. This fuel gas is an unstable compound or mixture of oxygen and fuel which burns above the wood, producing heat and pressure much slower than a chemical explosion. A detonation may take place in a split second, producing

Figure 28. A vacuum effect occurred when a bomb exploded in a parking lot just to the right of this building. As a result, the vacuum effect pulled the windows straight out of the building for 50 feet in the direction of where this photograph was taken.

sudden pressure. A fire has three requirements: fuel, oxygen and initiation. The same is true of an explosion as seen in Figure 29. The initiation has three requirements: the flame, fire, sparks or heat must be of high enough temperature, sufficient duration and cover enough area.

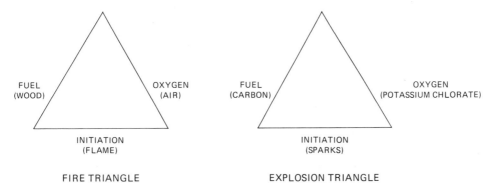

Figure 29. Simple fire triangle, well known to all fire fighters, is applicable to explosives as well. Previously unpublished is the fact that the initiation has three requirements. The heat must be of sufficient temperature, sufficient duration and cover sufficient area.

Any explosive must contain its own oxygen to be defined as an explosive. It cannot draw its oxygen from the air, as wood does when it burns. An explosive must be sensitive to initiation by heat or pressure (shock).

In the production of an explosive, fuel is mixed with oxygen. For example, gasoline itself is not explosive, but gasoline vapors are. Mechanical mixtures, such as black powder, are a combination of potassium nitrate for oxygen, sulfur for initiation and charcoal for fuel. In an explosive compound, oxygen is added to fuel through a nitration process. For instance, in the manufacture of nitroglycerine, a glycerine is placed with acids rich in oxygen: sulfuric acid (H_2SO_4) and nitric acid (HNO_3). The chemical reaction causes the glycerine to pull the oxygen out of the acid. This is true of other explosives, such as a mixture of toluene with acids to form trinitrotouene or of formaldehyde and ammonia with acids to form RDX. RDX is mixed with plasticizers to become composition C4, or plastic explosive.

INITIATION OF EXPLOSIVES

Some explosives are so sensitive to heat that they explode as a result of being mixed together. This is called being hypergolic. Red phosphorus and potassium chlorate are hypergolic. Black powder is sensitive to heat from a spark. Nitroglycerine requires pressure or shock. Nitro carbo nitrate requires more pressure than nitroglycerine.

Confining a lower-velocity explosive increases the velocity of the explosion. There is a cycle: the greater the heat, the greater the pressure; the greater the pressure, the greater the heat. Black powder or dynamite can be burned unconfined. All that black powder needs to make it explode is the confinement of a cardboard container. A steel pipe causes more heat and more pressure than cardboard before it breaks, and that is the reason black powder is used in pipe bombs. Smokeless powder confined in a can will merely burn, but when confined in a pipe, it will explode.

Heat and pressure in rockets escape through the venturi, but if the heat and pressure do not escape fast enough, the rocket explodes.

The Institute of the Makers of Explosives requires that dynamite be cap-sensitive and that it contain at least 12 percent nitroglycerine.

There are two types of blasting caps: electric and fuse. They contain a heat-sensitive explosive with a base charge susceptible to the pressure from the heat-sensitive explosive.

INITIATION OF BOMBS

A bomb is a device designed to explode in a specific manner. A bomb can be an explosive substance which is delivered with the unlawful intention of causing injury, death, destruction of property or creating a disturbance. A bomb may be delivered (planted or set) by being placed, dropped, thrown or projected.

The proper name for a bomb or initiating device that is not factory-made for commercial or military purpose is debatable. "Homemade" does not accurately describe a bomb made by someone in his own shop or office or in a field. "Fabricated" means manufactured. "Improvised" is composed without preparation and is the word used by special forces. Now the term for a homemade bomb is an "improvised explosive device," or IED, as shown if Figure 30. An unidentified object that is thought to be a bomb is known as a ·suspected improvised explosive device, or SIED. It is treated as a bomb, or IED, until proven otherwise through investigation.

A limpit mine is an explosive charge that is attached with adhesive, tape, magnets or chain to a target such as ships or fuel-storage tanks.

For dismantling purposes, bomb technicians or specialists refer to a bomb as an "open bomb" if the means of initiation and explosive can be seen and a "closed bomb" if the component parts are covered in a container. With a closed bomb, it is difficult to determine at first whether or not it actually is a bomb. A partly open bomb has some of its components visible, usually enough to see that it is a bomb, but how to dismantle it or what to do with it is another question as shown in Figure 31.

An instructor in the Ku Klux Klan lectured to the members that a bomb is a good weapon for two reasons: a good bomb destroys all the evidence, and the perpetrator can be miles away when it explodes. He did not mention the disadvantage that often occurs—an innocent person such as a child may be near a time bomb at the moment it explodes, or an innocent person may explode a booby-trap bomb. Ed Yallop, MBE, worked at Woolwich Arsenal for years examining bomb evidence in the United Kingdom. He is the author of *Explosion Investigation* and strongly disagrees that a good bomb blows up all of the evidence. Mr. Yallop has spent many years finding evidence from bombings.

Bombs have three methods of being initiated. (Incidentally, *initiated* is the proper term, not *ignited,* since to ignite means to light.) These three

Figure 30. The author is shown finishing the dismantling of one of the most ingenious homemade bombs ever encountered. This radio-controlled torpedo was to be used on a British ship carrying buses to Cuba.

methods are: (a) time, (b) action or motion, and (c) command or remote control.

The time bomb is the most common bomb used in the United States. There are four types of time delays: (a) burning, (b) corrosive, (c) electrical, and (d) mechanical.

Burning black powder is the most common type of delay. The military MIAI corrosive delay firing device or time pencil shown in Figure 32 has been used at least twenty-seven times in the Dade County area but has not been used in any other area of the United States. Gerd Ester, of the German Bundeskriminalamt, found through research that a captured British time pencil was used in the 1944 assassination attempt of Hitler.

The homemade corrosive delay is usually an acid eating through a metal, or other separating medium, to a chemical that explodes on contact with the acid in a hypergolic reaction.

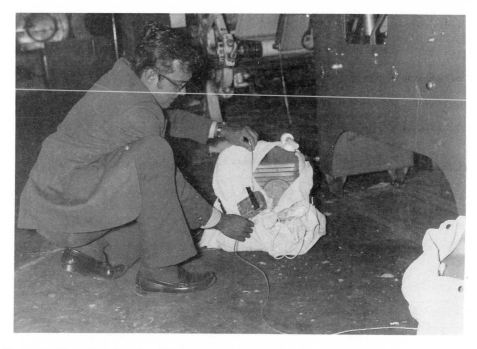

Figure 31. Metro Dade bomb technician, Dominic Gerard, is shown completing the dismantling of a combination improvised explosive and incendiary device. Several cans of gasoline were connected with some detonating cord.

The electrical time bomb is one of the most dangerous to dismantle when it incorporates a relay held in place by a battery. This is called a collapsing circuit, battery decay or a relay device. The first known design was by a Cuban, in Miami, and later placed on ships by terrorists in the Caribbean and Canada. One of these improvised explosive devices, as shown in Figure 33, was dismantled by the author in 1968. Allen Ferraday, OBE, dismantled the first E cell bomb, which is a sophisticated electronic timing device.

The mechanical delay is the second most common timing method and it is found in the form of a clock or watch. There are several methods of using this mechanism in a firing system. It is usually incorporated into an electrical system with a battery, and electric blasting cap or model rocket igniter. Most of the American casualties in Vietnam were caused by booby traps. In the United States, booby trap bombs are rarely encountered. A package bomb (a closed bomb) is just a portable booby trap. Beginning bomb squads and instructors tend to overemphasize "hands-on" methods of dismantling suspected improvised explosive devices

Figure 32. Q (Questioned) indicates fragments from the first time pencil used in the Miami area. At the center the complete pencil is shown and S (Standard) is the identified parts. A bomber in Miami told the author that his hair turned gray everytime he squeezed the pencil and then pulled out the safety band. The author dismantled three of the time pencil bombs.

or package bombs with hand-held tools. Although bomb squads have to deal with a lot of suspicious unidentified items, disrupters, robots and other remote dismantling procedures should receive the first consideration. Although hand-dismantling techniques should be practiced, they are only used as a last resort on actual suspected improvised explosive devices. Bomb disposal technicians should always remember that action-initiated bombs have been made to intentionally kill police.

The types of motion are three-dimensional—up, down, right, left, forward or backward. A combination of directions may be needed; i.e. twist or tilt, as in unwrapping a package or unscrewing a lid. Depending on the type of initiation needed for the switch or explosive, the motion may need to be fast for impact or friction as demonstrated in Figure 34. The action or motion can be slow, as in turning a mercury switch. The armed forces of the major countries manufacture demolition firing devices. One American multi-purpose item replaces four older ones. These military booby traps vary but are primarily of four actions: (a) pull, (b) tension release, (c) pressure and (d) pressure release. All of these devices can be improvised.

The third method of initiation is by command or remote control and

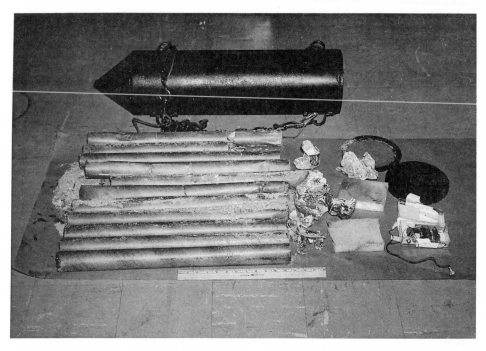

Figure 33. This bomb was removed from a British ship by Officer Ed Zehnder after five dives. The author dismantled this first recovered relay-initiated bomb.

it normally is initiated by one of four methods: (a) electronic, (b) electrical as shown in Figure 35, (c) mechanical, and (d) projectile. This type of initiation has been used for assassination because the bomber can make sure his victim is near the bomb before he explodes it. However, it requires that the bomber or his observer be in the proximity of the scene. Radio or other types of transmitters can produce an electronic impulse to explode a bomb. Some of the problems with electronically controlled bombs are: (a) extraneous signals on the same frequency, (b) interference by other electronics, (c) static electricity or heavy electrical power sources that are nearby, (d) intentional jamming of frequencies, and (e) body or metal interference.

A concealed dual electric wire to a concealed bomb can be exploded by a bomber with a battery or other power source. If the wire is then recovered by the bomber, there will be less evidence.

Mechanically remote control bombs can be exploded by pulling a long string or wire. Bullets or other projectiles can be used to impact with a bomb in place. Bombs that are projected, thrown or dropped often are initiated by impact which may be classified as a command form of initiation.

Figure 34. The author is shown pulling a commercial friction pull fuse lighter on a Cuban homemade grenade. These pull wires have been found twice at bombings in the Miami area.

VARIATIONS IN BOMBS

"What does a bomb look like?" is a question frequently asked by the general public who may be potential victims of bombings. The answer is, "A bomb can look like anything." Persons who are concerned about their own safety, or the search for bombs, or have to be alert to prevent bombs from being brought into an area, will be safer after acquiring the following information on differences in bomb appearance. Identification through recognition aids in bomb security and is an important factor in keeping bomb disposal technicians alive. Identification through recognition helps investigators gather evidence to prevent future bombings.

An axiom of bomb disposal technicians is that the improvisation of a bomb is limited only by the ingenuity of the maker. Variations in bombs depend on two factors: the bomber and the target. The bomber may be male or female. The bomber may act alone or with a group. Motives and intentions influence the type of bomb that is used. Motive is the reason

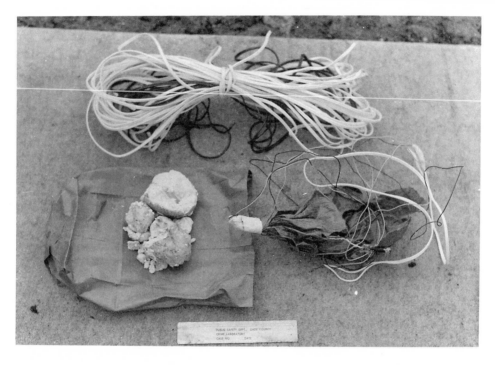

Figure 35. This electrical command or remote-control bomb was dismantled at police head-quarters after a police officer brought it into the office. If an officer is advised that an object is a bomb, the area should be evacuated and a bomb squad requested to investigate the object.

for the bombing. Intentions refer to how many casualties, how much damage or the message the bomber wishes to deliver.

In recent years, the Federal Bureau of Investigation and the Bureau of Alcohol, Tobacco and Firearms have studied the motives, intent and characteristics of bombers. This computerized information is applied to the investigation of the present cases, intelligence gathering and bomb protection of possible future targets. Intelligence information is merely investigation before a crime occurs, in order to prevent the crime from being committed or apprehend the perpetrators.

The most common ways to obtain explosives or any other bomb components are by stealing, buying or making them. These three sources, combined with the next five, are a complete list of sources of all materials: to find, receive, trade, mine or grow from plant or animal life.

One of the principles of bomb protection is to cut off, limit, control or regulate the sources of explosives or other bomb-making materials.

Besides explosives, or chemicals to manufacture explosives, many other materials may be used in factory manufacturing or improvisation of bombs or explosive devices. These materials may include electrical and electronic components. By tracing the components to the source, distributor or manufacturer, the bomb protection specialist may be able to determine how to interdict bombs before the bombs are even made.

The areas where bombs are made and where materials are stored before and after they are made and the methods of transportation influence differences in bombs. The tools that are used in the manufacture of any part of a bomb also may be gathered by one person, improvised into a bomb by a second person and delivered to a target by a third person.

When protecting a target, it is advisable to do a survey and try to determine the means and route by which the bomber is to arrive and leave. Bomb protection personnel should try to decide if the method used will be a huge truck with tons of explosives, a four-ounce letter bomb, a sniper with a rocket-launched missile or any of the above.

Containers

A knowledge of the reasons for bomb containers will help a person identify possible bombs while guarding or searching an area. This is important for a bomb disposal technician or an investigator in a post-blast search.

Every bomb must have an explosive and a means of initiation, but they do not necessarily always have a container. A bomb container may be a cover, a binder, a chassis or frame. A bomb container may serve more than one purpose, at different times, for the same bomb. The following reasons for bomb containers may be used for a checklist:

1. The main reason for a bomb container may simply be to hold the bomb or any of its parts together, or to connect to other bombs. This may include the initiation system or other parts of the container. Tape, string, glue, adhesive, bags, boxes, pipes and luggage are all commonly used in improvised as well as factory-manufactured bombs.

2. Confinement by a container will increase velocity of any explosive that burns at less than 16,000 feet per second. This is a very common reason for utilizing steel or plastic pipe-bomb containers. A pipe bomb may be within or attached to another type of container. An initiation system may be totally within a pipe or partially outside a pipe container.

3. Concealment is a common reason for containers or covers for bombs.

The cover is targeted or a duplicate of part of the target area, i.e., a box similar to other boxes stored at the site. In Haiti, the author dismantled the bomb shown in Figure 36. The bomb was concealed in a tape recorder which was in a cardboard box, wrapped in brown paper and shipped on a Pan American airliner.

Figure 36. After one bomb exploded in a Pan American freight warehouse in Haiti, a second bomb was found by checking the cargo manifest. The author dismantled this bomb with the aid of x-ray.

4. Fragmentation may be the main reason for a bomb container to create more damage or injuries. Fragmentation from a bomb is called primary fragmentation. Fragmentation from the environment, target or location where a bomb is exploded is called secondary fragmentation. Shrapnel is extra material in addition to the bomb container for the purpose of causing additional casualties or damage.

5. Incendiary materials may be part of a container designed to create a hotter and larger flame to ignite flammable material or cause fire

casualties. Flammable is the correct term for the susceptibility of material to burn. (Inflammable refers to infection.)

6. Destruction of evidence may be a purpose of a container or cover by a bomber. The obliteration of fingerprints by painting a bomb may be a prime example.

7. Transportation of a bomb may result in containers that are bags and luggage. Aerial bombs and rockets may have propulsion systems, guidance systems and may have ballistic shaped containers. Figure 37 shows a bomb similar to one that terrorist bombers from Miami used to bomb a Soviet ship in Havana Harbor.

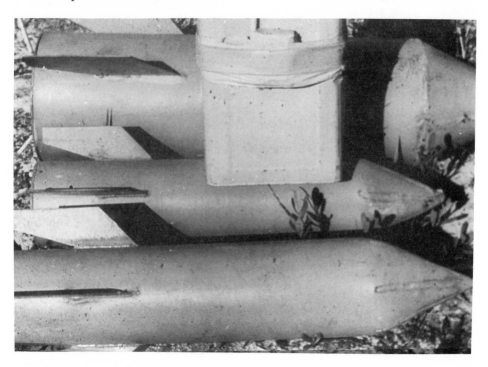

Figure 37. The container of this largest bomb is similar to the container of the bomb shown in Figure 33, except this bomb has tail fins to be used as an aerial bomb, and of course it was built by the same bombers.

8. Insulation from weather or shock may result in a container being used to prevent vibration, temperature extremes of heat or cold, electronic radiation, rain, snow and dirt from prematurely initiating a bomb or interfering with the sensitivity of the explosive. An insulator from shock is illustrated in Figure 38.

9. Attachment of a bomb to a target produces odd pieces of evidence at

Figure 38. A cardboard box filled with shredded paper was found near the crater. The easiest access to the target was by boat and the bomber may have used the box of paper as insulation against vibration during delivery.

the scenes of bombings. Officer Ed Zehnder of the Metro Dade Police Department removed a 45-pound bomb from the bottom of a ship where it had been attached with a chain and a padlock.

10. The container may serve as part of the initiation system of a bomb, as the fuze does in a hand grenade. (In military nomenclature, fuse is spelled with a "z," and commercially, fuse is spelled with an "s.") Other parts of the grenade container serve multiple purposes: to hold the grenade together, fragmentation, delivery, insulation, identification, ballistics, directional effects, storage, attachment, concealment and/or transportation.

11. The safety may be part of the container. Some bombs may have safeties and they are usually found near the outside or top of the bomb or just inside the cover.

12. Identification of a bomb may be the only reason or one of the reasons for a bomb container. The armed forces use color markings as well as writing in different forms for ammunition handlers. Improvised explosive devices as well as hoax devices may be marked to warn or scare people or draw more victims to the scene. Instructions have been found on some bomb containers.

13. Misinformation may be written on a container as instructions to a potential victim, to have him open a bomb to initiate it.

14. Directional shaping of the effects of a bomb may be the object of the bomb maker to send the maximum effects of an explosion in one direction for penetration of a target barrier or to reach a distant target.

15. Attenuation, or mitigation, are terms for lessening the effects of an explosion and may be the purpose of a bomb container.

16. The bomber may place a cover, or container, on a bomb to make it more difficult or easier to dispose of a device. The land mines that were once used along the Iron Curtain had their fuzes replaced periodically for maintenance purposes.

INCENDIARIES

What to call a "molotov cocktail" is a question that has been discussed frequently. Explosives Officer Al Gleason of the Bureau of Alcohol, Tobacco and Firearms compiled an explanation of the United States law pertaining to the "Destructive Devices and Explosives" definitions in 1977. Officer Gleason's interest led to research of congressional legislative history regarding these laws. Based upon his research, he concluded that Congress, in writing the Title XI Explosives Law, intended to include within the explosive definition just about anything that might cause an explosion.

Al Gleason analyzed the part of the law that states, "Any chemical compound or mechanical mixture, or device that contains any oxidizing and combustible units, or other ingredients, in such proportions, quantities or packing that ignition by fire, by friction, by concussion, by percussion or by detonation of the compound mixture or device or any part thereof, may cause an explosion." The phrases, "Any chemical compound or mechanical mixture that . . . in such proportions . . . that ignition by fire . . . may cause an explosion," convinced Officer Gleason that this would include flammable liquids such as gasoline. Seeing as how flammable liquids are often used as accelerants in arson, Officer Gleason felt that the BATF would in some cases have jurisdiction and justification for the investigation of arson.

That was the beginning, and the BATF made and prosecuted many of those cases. In 1982, based upon the BATF's successful arson programs, the law was changed to include all types of arsons that fell within the federal area of jurisdiction.

BOMB EXPERT OPINION

In a bombing, the expert may have to testify that what had occurred was not an accidental explosion but had been caused by a bomb. In order to do this, the expert must have a pre-trial conference with the attorney so as to be thoroughly prepared. Examination of reports, evidence, preparation of illustrations, including charts, testing, reproduction of explosive effects and dummy exhibits may all be in order.

The expert should have prepared questions and answers which will gradually show why his background entitles him to give the opinion required by the attorney. The expert must be prepared to defend his opinion to the opposing attorney and to the judge.

Chapter 5

EXPLOSIVE AND BOMB LAWS

PURPOSE

Control of explosives will lessen the chances of bombings in your jurisdiction or in neighboring jurisdictions. This precept is as fundamental to police as is the knowledge that if cars are locked it will lessen the chance of their being stolen. It is as fundamental to fire fighters as is the knowledge that if a building follows the fire code rigidly, it lessens the chance of a fire fatality as shown in Figure 39.

Figure 39. Just after fire fighters arrived at a burning house, an illegal, unknown cache of dynamite exploded, flattening the fire fighters and disintegrating the burning house. If it is known that dynamite is burning, fire fighters should not attempt to extinguish the blaze because burning dynamite sometimes will explode.

The main methods that bombers use to obtain explosives are by stealing, buying or making them. If there are lax regulations regarding explosives, it is easier for a bomber to buy explosives. Formerly, some states only required a purchaser to give his name, and dealers stored dynamite with caps under the counter inside hardware stores. One of the principles of bomb protection is to interdict the bomber's source of explosives and other bomb-making materials.

REGULATIONS FOR EXPLOSIVES

The main commercial explosives used are slurries, water gels and nitro carbo nitrate. Dynamite is still used but in limited amounts.

New York City has the most stringent regulations on the use of explosives. All sticks of dynamite must be numbered. All handlers of explosives must be licensed. All places where dynamite is stored must have a watchman on duty twenty-four hours a day. In 1955, as a result of a series of synagogue and racial bombings, the Dade County Sheriff's Office and the Florida State Fire Marshal wrote and sponsored some of the best state laws and regulations on the control of explosives. Dade County restricts the use of explosives even more, while Miami Beach prohibits the use of any explosives whatsoever.

Dade County was one of the first places in the world that prohibited the use of safety fuse and fuse caps in blasting. This was a result of two industrial blasting accidents in which three men were killed, not as a fault of the fuse, but as a result of using too short a length of fuse. This was contrary to safety precautions advised by fuse manufacturers, as shown in Figures 40, 41, 42 and 43. Since 1958, Dade County required fingerprints and photographs of all applicants for blasting permits. A blaster must take a written examination to prove that he is competent in the use of explosives. Laws governing the use of explosives are the same as any other law, in that those which cannot be enforced due to a lack of sufficient personnel to enforce them do not solve the problem.

Every time there is a theft of explosives, the authorities should make every effort to recover it or solve the theft before the explosives are used in a bombing. At the height of Cuban terrorist activity in South Florida, 50 percent of the thefts resulted in local bombings and 50 percent of the explosives were destined for Cuba as shown in Figures 44 and 45. Most of those shipments were intercepted by customs agents, as shown in Figure 46. In most areas of the country, 90 percent of dynamite thefts result in

Figure 40. Careless use of explosives resulted in the victim's decapitation.

Figure 41. Examination of remains of victims may indicate their position at the time of the explosion. Careful interpretation and training may prevent future accidents.

Figure 42. This victim had been facing the explosives which were about four feet above the ground. The object of any bombing or explosion investigation is to prevent more of the same from occurring.

Figure 43. Blasting caps stored with dynamite is a safety violation. The cause of deaths of the victims shown in Figures 40, 41, and 42 was six-inch lengths of fuse.

bombings. Just as a good detective knows that every armed robbery case is a potential homicide, he must also realize that every dynamite theft or case of illegal possession of explosives is a potential bombing. Every community government should have good laws regulating the type and amount of explosive used, safe handling and storage facilities. Millions of pounds of explosives are used in Dade County every year to make canals, fill low land, make cement and form road bases. Even though the regulations are strict, careless use of explosives have caused seven accidents and one bombing which resulted in thirteen deaths in 20 years as shown in Figure 47.

Figure 44. A university student who worked his way through college as a bank robber points to dynamite he stole to use on armored cars. Other members of the gang threatened to kill him, so he was forced to call the police to save his life.

The following provisions are given as possible examples for other areas. Section 13 of the Code of Metropolitan Dade County deals with the use of explosives. In order for a person to purchase explosives, the distributor must see the user's permit, write the number of the permit on the receipt and submit a copy of the receipt to the fire marshal within twenty-four hours.

The blaster must be careful to limit the quantity of explosive. When a permit is obtained, the fire marshal determines the amount to be used in

Figure 45. Shown are 75 cases of stolen dynamite that was hidden in a ravine and covered with mats by a thief who only wanted to obtain a little dynamite. He wanted to blow up a detective who had shot him previously but instead decided to fill his truck. He was arrested while attempting to find Cuban customers in bars. This type of theft and bar solicitation has occurred at least twice in South Florida.

individual blasts to prevent complaints from neighbors. The blaster must keep records of the amounts used in each shot.

A formula was set up by seismologist consultants to prevent excessive ground vibrations. The reading of a seismograph must not exceed an energy ratio of 1.0. Energy ratio $= (a^2/f^2) = 10.8f^2A^2$ in which a is the acceleration (acceleration of gravity, feet per second), f is the frequency (cycles per second) and A is the amplitude (inches).

The law enforcement officer is in the middle in blasting complaints. The complainant makes exaggerated claims of damage. However, if he had not heard the sound of the blast many times, the complainant probably would not have realized that there was any damage to his building.

The explosive companies claim that ground vibrations make X-type cracks in buildings, while settling causes linear or vertical cracks. Actually the cracks in structures are caused by settling, and eventually, through the years, a building will keep cracking until it falls down. However, ground vibration expedites the settling process.

Figure 46. United States Customs Officers, Coast Guard and other law enforcement agencies recovered over 4,000 bombs and tons of explosives from terrorist groups in South Florida which the author destroyed.

Bombing Statutes

Chapter 552 of the Florida State Statutes prohibits the possession or transportation of explosives without a license. A violation of this law is a felony.

Chapter 790 calls for the death penalty for throwing bombs in a public place or throwing, placing, discharging or attempting to discharge a destructive device which results in death. Causing injury or damage to property are punishable by imprisonment. A threat to bomb a person or place is also a felony. A false report of a bomb is a different crime, depending on the wording used by the perpetrator.

Shooting a deadly missile into buildings or vehicles can result in a loss of ten years of freedom for the convicted person. A missile is an object capable of being thrown or projected. Deadly means to be capable of inflicting a fatal injury.

The author helped write state statute 806.111 which prevents the possession, manufacture or disposal of a fire bomb with willful or mali-

Figure 47. Three deaths occurred as a result of 3,000 pounds of explosives being initiated by a sledge-hammer being used to try to remove 300 pounds of explosives from a drill tube.

cious intent to burn or set fire to a building or property. The fire bomb is defined as a breakable container which has flammable material with a wick.

Florida State Statute 790.165 prohibiting planting of "hoax bombs" is recent legislation. To fill a void, this legislation was drafted through the efforts of members of the Florida Chapter of the International Association of Bomb Technicians and Investigators. This is a model law which has been tested and used as a tool for law enforcement in Florida. Other agencies are now preparing similar laws in their respective jurisdictions.

Federal Regulations

The United States Code Title 18, Crimes and Criminal Procedures Part I, is the authority by which the interstate use of explosives is enforced by the Bureau of Alcohol, Tobacco and Firearms of the United States Treasury Department. The BATF has become more involved with assisting local and state law enforcement agencies in the last two decades. They helped provide a ready and valuable assistance that was needed in many cases where local laws and services are limited.

Chapter 6

BOMB SEARCH PROCEDURES

A bomb scare is a report of a bomb or a threat to bomb. The report may be false or real. A false report of a bomb with intent to deceive or a threat to bomb property or a person are felonies in Florida. The wording that a suspect uses will determine the charges to be placed against him. If the suspect states, "There is a bomb in your building," he is making a report. If the suspect states, "I am going to bomb your building," it is a threat.

Every bomb report or threat should be treated as real until reasonable investigation and search of the threatened location proves the message is false or fails to disclose a bomb.

There are four problems to be considered in the preparation of any tactical plan concerning bomb scares: evacuation, search, disposal (discussed in Chap. 7) and investigation.

EVACUATION

Police and management once believed that the location of the bomb scare should always be evacuated. Experience has taught that the decision to evacuate is different in each bomb scare. New York City and London, where there have been more bomb scares than most other jurisdictions, have developed the employee search plan. In 1973, this author described the employee search plan in the *MTI Bombs Familiarization and Bomb Scare Planning Workbook*, published by Motorola Telprograms, Inc. The book is now out of print. There is no constitutional law that gives the police the right to forcibly evacuate a building or to search it without a warrant. Some laws are open to debate: failure to obey a police officer in the performance of his duty, deputizing the manager, reason to believe a felony has been committed and emergency police powers in the event of a disaster. Also, the manager can be advised that if he does not evacuate the building and a bomb explodes, he may be civilly liable or held responsible for negligence in manslaughter charges. The best method, however, is establishing good rapport by being tactful.

If the authorities demand that the location be evacuated in every bomb scare, they may find that the manager will not call them the next time he receives a call. This is self-defeating to the proper protection of life and property. One of the causes of a bomb-scare call is to hurt the target financially by causing loss in business during the time of evacuation or by causing customers to change to a competitive business because of fear. If a business is forced to evacuate daily, it may become bankrupt because of large financial losses from lack of business during the time of evacuation.

In clearing a building, the occupants may be placed in greater jeopardy while they are leaving than if they stayed where they were. Most bombs are on the outside of a building, near the entrance or on the first floor. While leaving, the occupants would be passing by the best possible location of a bomb.

Evacuation depends on many factors. Good intelligence information, planning, training and cooperation are the primary tools to facilitate the decision to evacuate. If these tools are not used, the decision to evacuate or not may be erroneous and lead to panic, confusion, injuries and loss of valuable time, property and business.

The responsibility for the decision to evacuate is usually that of the local law enforcement agency and the management of the location in question. Evaluation of the bomb scare, or bomb threat, depends upon the information that is received on that particular incident and information that is known of other scares and bombings. If the number of anonymous calls that are received in a particular jurisdiction are in the vicinity of a hundred a day, then it may be impossible to send a police officer to respond to each scene. It may then be the decision of the manager of each location whether to evacuate or not.

On the other hand, the local police may have good information that a bomb is definitely at the location in question and demand evacuation immediately or at a particular time. Several factors are helpful in evaluation of the decision to evacuate: if the place or an associate has been bombed before that time, if the information gives the exact location and description of the bomb and the exact time of day, or a particular key word or phrase is part of the message of previous actual bombings.

Evacuation is best performed when it is known exactly where a suspect bomb is and the approximate size of the bomb. The occupants may be safer if employees examine their own area to make sure there is no bomb in their vicinity.

To safely evacuate large skyscrapers, auditoriums, stadiums or hospitals in a short time is a very difficult task. To advise all occupants of a bomb scare and order them to evacuate may create panic and injuries. The decision to evacuate should be coordinated with a staff of employees who have been trained to make sure there are no suspicious objects in their work areas.

The purpose of evacuation in a bomb scare or threat is to safely move the people away from a bomb. The purpose of a search for a bomb during a bomb scare is to determine if a bomb may exist and the location of the bomb. If the location of a possible bomb is not known at the time of an evacuation, it is difficult to determine which way to go to get away from it.

Evacuation during every bomb scare or threat may be self-defeating. The anonymous telephone bomb scare caller, or other persons, may be encouraged to call as often as he or she wishes. Evacuation, disruption of business, attention to a cause or terror may be the caller's only object.

Evacuees should know all exits and alternate exits in the event of a suspect item being found along a particular route. Gathering points for evacuees must be designated and should also be searched for suspect bombs. Alternate gathering points for evacuees may have to be planned that are safe from bombs, snipers or the elements.

Evacuation may be in different forms: (1) mandatory of the entire area in every bomb scare or threat, (2) complete evacuation only if a code word is given by a bomb scare caller, (3) partial evacuation always, and (4) partial evacuation only if a suspect item is found and depending upon the size and possible effects of a bomb and the barriers of the facility.

Good planning and training will not only save lives, time, business and property but will also raise morale and relieve anxiety from bomb scares or threats.

SEARCH

Searching techniques on bomb scares and bomb threats have changed throughout the years. Too often, equipment has greatly improved while some people still remain rigid in unnecessarily risking their lives without adopting methods that have been proven effective.

Management, fire and police officials are still using police officers to search for bombs during bomb scares. Fire fighters are being brought in and occupied during bomb scares, leaving some areas in their jurisdictions less protected. The largest air disaster with the biggest loss of life and property was caused by a bomb scare. The main airport in the Azores was closed due to a bomb scare, and aircraft were rerouted to an alternate airport without proper air traffic control. The result was a mid-air collision.

Search teams may be brought into a location to do bomb searches during a scare. The problem is obtaining sufficient search personnel who are familiar with the area and search procedures. Team searching may require long periods of evacuation of all employees or may be done while employees, customers or patients are still at the location.

Some management and public safety officials have chosen not to search during a bomb scare or to even notify employees that a bomb scare has been received. This course of action leaves those responsible for nonfeasance and may be open for union grievances. The writer has testified in such an arbitration hearing. Management lost, but all involved welcomed the employee search training.

Searching a location for a bomb is best performed by occupants of the building. They know the location and can tell immediately that no unusual objects are in their particular area. A good public relations program can teach the owners, managers or occupants of all large potential bombing sites what to do in the event of a bomb scare. This is done for several reasons: to protect life and property, to save time in the search, to prevent panic and loss of business and to apprehend the suspect so he will not be making any more calls. If it is explained to employees in staff meetings why their assistance is requested in searching, they are usually happy to be helpful. Employees at the location must be strongly advised not to touch anything if they do not know what it is. Employees have keys to locked doors and are familiar with objects and construction of buildings. A public safety representative would take much longer to search an area with which he is not familiar. Custodians or maintenance men at the location are also very helpful in searching.

Command Post

A floor plan of the entire area to be searched should be examined at a central command post where telephones are available. Of course, sometimes this may be the most likely area to be bombed. If there is an intercommunication system, then a predetermined code may be arranged with employees so that they will search their room or area, lock the door and evacuate, if that is the desired procedure. From the command post, other areas are assigned to be searched, which will insure that all sections are searched and that no time is wasted searching some areas several times.

Communications

With a good public address system and telephones, large skyscrapers or facilities can be completely searched in a reasonable manner within fifteen minutes. Evacuation of an area that size is difficult to accomplish in the same time.

Years ago, the procedure was setting up a command post a block away from a bomb scare area and evacuating the area to avoid initiation of a possible bomb by radios. If this is done, communications within the area is seriously handicapped so that some employees are not able to be notified that a bomb scare exists. The command post should be set up where there is the best communications. The Institute of the Makers of Explosives set up the safe distance for radio transmitters and electric blasting caps at 250 feet. The safe distance is actually much shorter than this. Radio receivers are much safer than transmitters. In this case, only electric blasting caps are affected and dynamite, fuse caps, detonating cord, black powder and all other explosives are not. A radio-controlled bomb can be set off by police or fire communications frequencies. Hand-carried radios are often used in searches, but for the best policy, it would be best not to use them.

Electric blasting caps are manufactured in an accordion fold and the leg wires shunted (shorted together) to prevent static electricity and radio waves from detonating the caps. In this condition they can be carried in vehicles, next to radios which are in use.

Radio communication also brings up the point of publicity. The more the public hears about bombs, the more false calls and threats may be received. Authorities can be notified by telephone, rather than the call being given over the radio for the news media to monitor.

Training

Good management, administration and supervision policies dictate that it is best to have a meeting with employees to explain any change when major operational procedures are planned. The best method is to introduce the employee search plan to employees one day during roll call with all employees present. Memorandums or written bulletins before a meeting is held may tend to cause misunderstanding and confusion and should be avoided. If unions are involved, it is best to have a discussion with any of the shop stewards and union representatives prior to the meeting being held, in order to obtain their support.

The employees are first advised of the problem that bomb scares or threats create. Employees should also be made aware of the number of bomb scares and bombings that do occur. The main purpose of bomb protection plans is to save lives. Secondary purposes of bomb protection plans would be to increase morale to employees by their knowing that search plans are the safest means of coping with the problem. Saving business, employment, time and property are the tertiary purposes of bomb protection planning. Employee search plans are merely self-help in making certain that each employee is safe from bombs. Bomb protection plans also include security by making the employees aware of preventive measures.

Employees realize that no one knows their work areas as well as they do. Employees become alert to anything strange or out of place. Unknown objects in their area may then become suspect items. The employees become security conscious. In the event of an anonymous telephone bomb scare, an employee would be able to advise what is suspicious and what is not.

In a bomb scare plan all areas are assigned to specific persons for searching. If some persons are not present, then alternate persons should be assigned. A bomb scare plan should be functional every hour of every day for every contingency. Backup personnel should be sent to areas when employees have not reported completion of their search.

The object of a bomb protection plan is to locate a possible bomb in an area so that employees, customers or patients may be evacuated to a place of safety. Since most bombs are located outside buildings or near doors, stairs, or halls, it is best to stay in a familiar work area where employees know there are no suspicious items. If all employees readily participate in the search and report their areas clear, then the employee search plan for bomb scares and bomb threats is the safest method to follow.

If an employee does not wish to participate in the search and wishes to evacuate, he or she should be given that choice but should be advised that he or she may be going to an area that has not been searched. Bombers may also place bombs in vehicles parked outside of buildings.

In an employee search plan, it is best to train every employee on every shift how to make sure there are no suspicious objects in the area where they work. They are trained not to touch suspicious objects and to notify the command post or communications center, of their facility, while evacuating their area.

Many employees may work in the same area eight hours a day, five days a week. The employees know what should be there and what should not be there. They know what doors and drawers have been locked or closed and how to obtain access to various areas. Employee search teams who may be sent into unknown areas may sometimes fail to identify what is suspicious and what is not.

The communications center should be contacted immediately by an employee, with an all-clear report if nothing suspicious is found. The command center then checks off the area on a list or floor plan. When every area is cleared, the command center can quickly ascertain that no suspect bomb is in the facility.

Employees are trained to realize that all bombs do not smoke or tick but may explode on time, motion or command. Employees are advised that most bombs are small and if there is no bomb in their immediate area, it is less dangerous to remain where they know there is nothing suspicious. If all employees search their area and immediately report their findings to the command post upon completion of their search, the sooner everyone will feel safe.

Most bombs are small enough to be hand-carried and will usually affect the room where the bomb is. If an employee does not find a suspicious object in his work area, he is usually safer to stay where he is and report by telephone, to the command, that his area is clear. If all employees do this, the area becomes secure more quickly. Intelligence information, distance and barriers are the first three principles of bomb protection. Knowledge of your facility and the thickness of walls, floors and roofs help encourage employees that these barriers help prevent bomb effects from penetrating their work areas. Even though the World

Trade Center bomb was estimated to be approximately 1,250 pounds of explosive, the primary effects were contained in the basement area.

Hand-carried bombs rarely exceed fifty pounds. A fifty-pound bomb usually affects the room it is located in, the two adjacent rooms on each side of that room, the room above the epicenter of the bomb and the room below the bomb. With this knowledge, evacuation from an area of a suspected bomb is usually three hundred feet away from the suspected item. Barriers consisting of walls, floors and roofs may shorten the distance of an evacuation from a fifty-pound bomb.

The most common places for bombs are the outside of a building, the entrance, the first floor, bathrooms, storerooms and waste receptacles. The custodians play a large part in searches, since they are familiar with, and have keys to, many rooms that are seldom used.

Bomb Drills

Immediately after the employee meeting, a scheduled bomb drill is held. Supervisors check on employees to make sure they search their areas and report their areas clear. Employees are advised that future bomb drills will not be scheduled in advance. There should be no panic or confusion in later bomb drills. If suspect items are found, then that area is immediately evacuated to await the arrival and disposal by the bomb disposal technicians.

Fire drills may be conducted to prevent panic during evacuations in the event of a real fire. Bomb drills may be conducted in a similar fashion.

In the event of a bomb scare that is deemed to be real or a suspect item is found, well-trained employees are able to leave that immediate area without unnecessary delay, panic or risk.

The key to an effective bomb scare plan is a communications system for instant notification of all employees. Employees must be able to communicate to the manager or the command post of a bomb scare or threat operation if suspect items are found in their area. Communications must have auxiliary generators for electric power. In the bombing of the New York World Trade Center, the explosion knocked out the water cooling supply for the emergency generators.

Employees are advised repeatedly not to touch anything suspicious but to evacuate the area and to advise the command post during a bomb scare. If a bomb disposal technician is brought in to search an area, it takes a much longer time for him to search the same area thoroughly because he is not familiar with the area. He may pass by some thing that is obviously out of place that an employee might immediately label as suspicious. Employees are better at examining their areas than bomb disposal technicians in reasonable searches.

Public Safety Departments

Public safety officials should always be advised of bomb drills beforehand. Public safety officials should be advised of bomb protection plans by large businesses. Police and fire officials are greatly relieved when businesses and schools develop their own employee search plans. When a police department may receive many bomb scare calls a day, then they may only be able to take reports by telephone or send one officer to take a report. If a suspected explosive device is located, the item should only be examined by a bomb disposal technician or his robot.

Bomb disposal technicians can serve and protect their jurisdictions more efficiently by introducing the employee search plan to all of the largest businesses, schools, hospitals and government agencies in their areas. Lives can be better protected and thousands of hours of time can be saved for other useful purposes. The morale of those served is increased by the employee search plan.

Once perpetrators see that an employee search plan does not cause the disruption of normal business, then the anonymous calls diminish considerably.

Police officers who are used in searches may have to leave their zones uncovered. This may be a reason for a bomb scare—so robberies can be committed elsewhere. Firemen are better than police for searching, because when they are not on a call, they are on standby at the firehouse. Also their ladders, tools, lights and other equipment may be needed for searching inaccessible places. Bomb squad personnel cannot quickly search large areas by themselves, but they should stand by for technical advise or until a suspected item is found.

The number of bombs that are found in bomb search cases are different, according to the situation. Ten percent is a high frequency rate, while one percent is low. If the caller describes the bomb, gives its location and gives his reason, you are more likely to find a bomb than if the caller simply states that there is a bomb.

A bomb hoax is an item which is made to look like a bomb. It may be marked "bomb" or like some type of explosive, or it may have warning messages on it. If the lettering is crude, it is more likely to be a hoax. A hoax item may contain an initiating device, but unless it contains an explosive, it cannot be classified as a bomb.

If a caller gives a time of explosion, this may shorten the time spent on a bomb search. In some instances, the authorities stand by after the specified time.

A department may decide that if a time is given, all searchers should leave the location during that time. However, if a large number of calls are received, this may not be practical.

Only the most obvious places can be searched for the most obvious bombs in a reasonable time. Examining each piece of furniture is often not practical. A bomb may be hidden between walls or buried among numerous containers, making a complete search impossible. When a search is completed, the manager or complainant should be told that after a thorough search a bomb *was not found.* Never advise him that it is perfectly safe or that there is no bomb.

Officials think in terms of a packaged time bomb when they are searching. But it may be a booby-trapped package or a booby trap attached to doors, lockers, furniture or windows, all of which must be searched. Unlatching and opening all doors by remote control with a string may not be possible. There is no absolutely safe way to handle all bomb situations. The use of a listening device in all areas or x-ray on all objects can be too painstaking a task when several bomb-scare calls are received daily.

Procedures of a public safety department will change with the type of area to be searched. Schools, hospitals, airplanes and automobiles all have individual problems. Searching school lockers is made easier if all padlocks are by the same manufacturer with an office master key for them. If the children are kept after school to make up for the evacuation time, it will sharply decrease the number of scares. Hospital patients may be alarmed by bomb scares. Formerly, in Dade County's largest hospital, the fire fighters wore laboratory jackets when assisting in searches. Now the hospital personnel perform searches more thoroughly without alarming patients or disrupting routine activities.

BOMB SECURITY

Bomb security measures are similar to other security measures but are conducted with the thought of preventing bombs from being delivered to a target. The employee search procedures can be applied for any target: individuals, groups of people, public places, modes of transportation, hospitals, schools, government buildings and businesses. These bomb protection measures are best explained to anyone involved, by a public awareness program. The program advises that the purpose of the measures are for their protection. The number of bomb scares or bombings or the possibilities of future incidents make certain precautions necessary.

Bomb security measures may cause certain areas to have restricted access. Locks, fences, checkpoints, surveillance cameras and guards may infringe on individual freedom or privacy because management or government wishes to protect the people.

In 1920, the explosion of a large bomb in a horse-drawn wagon in front of J.P. Morgan's offices at 23 Wall Street, New York City, killed thirty-eight people and wounded several hundred. This was the first known vehicle bomb. Since that time many different vehicle bombs have created security measures that prohibit leaving unattended vehicles in certain areas. Traffic congestion and travel have affected restricted parking areas so much that parking areas are being constructed under new buildings. Under-building parking facilities may increase the danger of a vehicle bomb's proximity to its target. This danger can be lessened by distance and barriers.

Access to buildings, airports and seaports requires restricting barriers and distance in future construction, as well as modifications to existing facilities. These restrictions impose on individual freedoms and comfort. An obvious bomb protection measure at airports and seaports is the removal of lockers from public access, unless the luggage stored in them is inspected first. However, some airports still have lockers even though airport lockers have been bombed in New York City, Los Angeles, Miami and other major cities.

Another simple bomb protection measure, that is necessary for ships and airliners, is to restrict luggage to hand-carried items weighing under forty pounds. For maximum security, all luggage should be opened to visual and olfactory inspection, as well as x-rayed by well-qualified and motivated employees. Passenger ships and passenger airplanes carry freight that is not closely examined for bombs. The solution may be simple, but again, individual freedom and expense are involved. Maximum security dictates that freight should not be shipped on vessels and airplanes that are allowed to carry passengers.

Airplane bomb scares can be handled in approximately one hour in the following manner. All passengers disembark from the aircraft. Airline personnel remove the luggage to luggage carriers. Two or three passengers at a time open their own suitcases in front of police officers. Airline personnel search the aircraft. Unclaimed freight is removed and held for twenty-four hours. This is not foolproof, but the search is reasonable without dismantling the aircraft. X-raying all of the suitcases is difficult and x-raying all of the freight may be close to impossible. Radiation exposure to operators, fogging of undeveloped film and time are a few of the problems encountered.

Public awareness programs will make bomb protection or security measures more easily acceptable.

The police officers and firemen should always bear in mind when searching that a false bomb report has preceded actual bombings at other times. In Dade County, Cuban bombers occasionally call the police if they have had a misfire. A warning call may be given to prevent innocent victims from being injured. Other callers may desire that police, firemen or victims be present and injured when a bomb does explode. The bomber may have just planted a bomb for an extortion and wants to make sure the recipient is aware that a bomb was planted.

INVESTIGATION

Bomb scares were popularized by George Metesky, the Mad Bomber of New York City. Metesky made anonymous reports, but he planted 33 bombs. False bomb reports and bomb threats are communicated in most cases by telephone and by an anonymous person. Most often the call may be received by an employee or inhabitant of the location, although the message is frequently received at the local fire or police agency.

Calls to fire and police station telephones are often taped. Some businesses have tape recorders that also can be used to provide permanent records of incoming or outgoing calls. The telephone company rents recorders that can be attached legally to a telephone. In addition, a new method has been developed by the telephone company to lock in on any call received at the complaint desk. The caller cannot call another number after his telephone has been locked in, but the complaint desk *can* call the individual back to verify an address or other information. With this method, the location of the telephone can always be traced after the suspect hangs up.

The recipient of a bomb scare call should normally ask the following questions in this order:

1. What is the exact location of the bomb?
2. What does the bomb look like?
3. What will make it explode?
4. How do we get rid of it?
5. Why did you put it there?

The person who receives such a call is often startled and does not think to obtain this valuable information from the anonymous caller. If the caller replies to these questions, time, lives and property can be saved.

Today, if recipients of annoying telephone calls make a request of their telephone company, future calls may be traced and recorded. If a person wishes to pay for the service, a customer may identify every number from which calls are made to his number.

The purpose of most anonymous bomb scare telephone calls is to cause annoyance while a location is evacuated and a search performed for a bomb. The most important question to ask is, "What is the exact location of the bomb?" If a suspicious item is found at that exact location, it is necessary to evacuate that area immediately. Since bombs are not all time bombs, the time it explodes is not always the first question to be asked. If it is known where the bomb is, then it is known which way to go to get away from it.

If, in fact, the caller has delivered a bomb to a target and it is a time bomb and he or she wishes to prevent injuries or fatalities, the caller will give the time and the exact location, if it is a large facility. If the anonymous caller does not specify the exact location of the bomb, then the purpose of the call is to cause the recipient(s) of the call to waste valuable time, risk lives and cause disruption. By all means, the most important information to know from an anonymous message concerning bomb scares is to know the exact location of the supposed bomb.

A recipient of an anonymous telephone bomb call should be questioned closely as soon as possible for information about the call. The exact words used by the caller are important, especially in determining a similarity to other bomb calls. A switchboard operator of a business establishment at times can tell from noises on the telephone if the call originated inside the building. Background noises, i.e. traffic, music and laughter, may be heard by the complainant, who may not volunteer the information unless specific questions are asked by the investigator to refresh his memory. The complainant may be able to give an opinion as to the sex, age, voice accent, attitude or a speech impediment of the speaker.

Voice-print identification can be of value in the investigation. Most telephone bomb calls are less than eight words. It is difficult to make a positive identification on less than eight words, but it may be helpful in elimination of a suspect. A voice on the telephone is more difficult to identify than a voice in person.

Oral messages delivered in person, such as passengers making "humorous" remarks to airline personnel about bombs, present no problems in solving. Flight personnel usually do not treat these sick jokes about bombs as humor. The comedian who makes statements about bombs at the airport may find himself under arrest by the Federal Bureau of Investigation and the flight delayed because of an ill-conceived remark.

Written messages are always better for police, since they provide possible fingerprint and handwriting identification.

Bomb searches can be very tedious and boring, but police officers and fire fighters should not become too blasé on this type of call, since the new threat of organized revolutionary groups planting bombs is to catch the officer unaware.

Chapter 7

BOMB DISPOSAL PROCEDURES

SOME ASPECTS OF THE PUBLICITY PROBLEM

This procedure will vary with the individual situation. A public safety department member called to a location where a suspected explosive or bomb is reported to be should notify the communications section of his findings. If possible, this should be done by telephone and not by radio, in order to avoid monitoring by news media. Publicity has advantages and disadvantages. Cooperation with the news media helps public relations and can assist in obtaining hazardous-duty pay and equipment for a bomb squad. News coverage will let the public know of your availability and may stimulate citizens to report storages of explosive or to report suspects. A disadvantage of publicity is that the more information the citizenry receives about bombs, the more it gives them ideas for false reports, threats and bombings and leads to experimentation with explosives by children.

DEVELOPMENT OF CIVILIAN BOMB SQUADS

Bomb squads that are established by police, fire or public works departments by national, state or local counties or cities are known as civilian bomb squads to differentiate them from the explosive ordnance disposal units that are formed by the armed forces of various nations.

The history of civilian bomb squads is also a study of bombings because bomb squads are developed as a result of necessity. The first known bomber was Guy Fawkes, who was arrested on November 4, 1605 by Sir Thomas Knyvet, who became the first known bomb squad commander. Guy Fawkes and others had placed barrels of gunpowder under the House of Lords in London to blow up the king and Parliament. Sir Thomas Knyvet acted on information received by Lord Monteagle, who became the first known bomb investigator. Sir Richard Walsh, the Sheriff of Worcestershire, arrested the other conspirators in what is now known as The Gunpowder Plot.

James McParlan was responsible for the arrest of the next recorded group of bombers, known as the Molly Maguires, in 1875. McParlan was an undercover private detective working for the Pinkerton Detective Agency.

An infamous bombing during a strike on May 4, 1886 killed seven police officers at Haymarket Square. An anarchist labor leader and three others were arrested and hanged.

Anarchist beliefs that people can live peacefully without government were developed and made explicit in writings by William Godwin and Pierre-Joseph Proudhon in 1840. Later anarchists were responsible for many assassinations through shootings and bombings. Among their victims were President Sadi Cannot of France in 1894, Empress Elizabeth of Austria in 1898, King Umberto I of Italy in 1900 and President McKinley in 1901.

The first police bomb squad, in 1903, was formed in New York City under Lieutenant Joseph Petrosino. The purpose was to combat the Black Hand, or Mano Nera, which was made up of several extortion rackets by Sicilians and Italians against merchants and well-to-do persons. They were threatened with death, injuries or property damage. Lieutenant Petrosino and his men sent many bombers to jail, or had them deported, before he was assassinated in Italy during an investigation. The New York City bomb squad has continued to be a model to this present day.

In 1908, in New York City, there was an attempt to blow up police during a demonstration at Union Square.

The Pinkerton Agency was responsible for the arrest of bombers in the Colorado area from 1903 to 1905. These bombers had killed a large number of miners and prominent individuals.

The Pinkerton Agency was responsible for the arrest and conviction of the McNamara brothers who bombed *The Los Angeles Times* newspaper on October 1, 1910.

The first description of a bomb disposal was in a Paris magazine depicting Monsieur Kling, of the Paris City Labortory, using an x-ray machine to dismantle two anarchists' bombs. This same year was the beginning of World War I. The assassination of the Archduke Ferdinand of Austria, which led to the beginning of the war, was preceded by a bomb.

In 1916, while President Wilson was giving a speech in New York City before a huge rally on war preparation, a labor union protest resulted in a large bomb explosion a few blocks away which killed nine people.

During World War II, there were a series of bombings in the New York area. The Black Tom explosion across the river in New Jersey was the largest explosion in the United States. The cause of this munitions shipping port disaster was never resolved.

In 1917, a bomb was brought into the Milwaukee Police Station. The premature explosion killed several officers. Milwaukee may have been the first equipped bomb squad in the United States, but there are no existing records of its existence.

In the early twenties, several bombings against government targets in Washington, D.C. occurred. The Burns Detective Agency was involved in some of the investigations and protection.

In 1922, a significant event in bombing investigation was the identification of a bomber, John Magnusson, through handwriting comparison. John F. Tyrrell was the prosecution's expert witness on this package bombing.

In 1927, James Belcastro was known as the King of the Bombers. He worked for Al Capone, blowing up saloons, polling places and the porches of politicians. The first crime laboratory in the United States was at Northwestern University. It was later given to the Chicago Police Department. Two of its members were Charles Wilson and Doctor Muhlberger. Charles W. Zmuda worked with them and later became an assistant chief of the Metro Dade Police Department. This author had the good fortune to learn under Zmuda's guidance and also attended a lecture by Doctor Muhlberger.

On July 4, 1940, at the New York World's Fair, two members of the New York City Bomb Squad were killed and two others permanently disabled while investigating a suspect bomb.

Due to the large number of recovered explosive devices in Dade County, Florida, I went to New York City to study for a week with its bomb squad. I also attended seven explosive reconnaissance courses given by the United States Armed Forces Explosive Ordnance Disposal Teams.

During the late sixties, Dade County received many inquiries regarding bombing incidents protesting the war in Vietnam. During this time, I taught police officers from several different states, other parts of Florida and as part of the International Police Academy.

Because of the bombings and violence in the late sixties, Senator

McClellan was chairman of a committee to attempt to help rectify the problem. As a result, three objectives were obtained: better federal laws regulating interstate transportation of explosives, the National Bomb Data Center (NBDC) and the Hazardous Devices School (HDS). At first, the NBDC was administered for the Department of Justice by the International Association of Chiefs of Police (IACP), and the Army conducted the HDS. Now, both programs are under the auspices of the Federal Bureau of Investigation.

In 1970, Thompson Crockett, of the International Association of Chiefs of Police, contacted me and asked to help assemble all of the bomb technicians in the United States. It was determined that there were only nineteen experienced civilian bomb disposal technicians in the United States, including nine from New York City. A preliminary seminar was held in Puerto Rico and the next meeting was at Dulles Airport. In attendance were Al Gleason of the New York City Bomb Squad, Ron Newhouser of the Air Force, Captain Bob Cote from Montreal, Bill Lee from Los Angeles, Bill Smith from Denver, Dewitt Moody from the Navy and Rod Jordan from Picatinny Arsenal.

In a series of meetings throughout the United States, we discussed training, equipment, procedures, communications and a future organization. James Bell, of the Ministry of Defense from the United Kingdom, hosted the first international conference on bombings. Sacramento Sheriff Duane Lowe hosted the first two meetings of the International Association of Bomb Technicians and Investigators.

Since the beginning of the HDS, over four thousand technicians have been trained.

The British Armed Forces Explosive Ordnance Disposal personnel did the bomb disposal for the United Kingdom, as they had done since the beginning of World War II. In 1963, New Scotland Yard initiated a bomb squad consisting of two men who were retired from the military EOD—Don Henderson and Geoffery Biddle. They were employed as a result of bombings by the Angry Brigade and approximately 500 yearly safe openings with explosives. Explosives used to open safes in the United States are rare. During a twenty-four-year time period in Miami, there were only six of these.

The German bomb disposal is performed by the public works department of each state. Not only do they dispose of over 450 tons of military ordnance a year, they also dispose of improvised explosive devices. Gerd

Ester, of the National Police, teaches bomb protection to all law enforcement personnel.

Bomb squads in small departments with limited funds depend on the individual initiative of its members. Sergeant Wayne Tanner, of the Saint John's County Sheriff's Office in St. Augustine, Florida, displays equipment that he has obtained using his ingenuity shown in Figure 48.

Figure 48. Some small bomb squads have very limited funds for equipment. Officers may depend on their own ingenuity and funds, appealing to the community and borrowing equipment.

The tragic bombing of the federal building in Oklahoma City in 1995 was a prime example of the progress of modern bomb methods and bomb protection methods. Ease of rapid transportation and communications present problems and assets to anyone concerned with bomb protection.

All of the principles of bomb protection listed in Chapter 11 can be demonstrated in the disastrous Oklahoma City incident. Intelligence information had been received that certain individuals were displeased with the federal government. Evaluation of this intelligence information may have led to further intelligence gathering, a change in federal policies, physical protection procedures, training, organization, equipment and personnel. Knowledge of bomb protection principles is essential in order to communicate these needs to superiors to convince them to provide finances for bomb protection.

Post-blast procedures require rapid response for personnel with heavy cranes and jacks to remove rubble in the search and rescue for survivors in the wreckage.

Rapid communications to establish roadblocks and a check of passengers at transportation terminals as soon as possible after a disastrous bombing usually occurs only when someone in authority grasps the magnitude of the situation and acts accordingly.

Since the training of thousands of bomb disposal technicians and post-blast investigators at Redstone Arsenal and the Federal Law Enforcement Training Center, there is no shortage of evidence-gathering personnel at bombings. Experience has taught the various agencies involved that mutual cooperation creates the best results.

Valuable lessons are to be learned from each incident and immediate results should increase all principles of bomb protection from establishing new laws to increased barriers for physical protection as shown in Chapter 11.

DUTIES OF THE FIRST OFFICER ON THE SCENE

The first public safety department officer on the scene should order the immediate evacuation of all persons to a place which is a safe distance from the bomb's suspected location. In determining the extent of evacuation required, it shall be assumed that a bomb or explosive may cause damage and fatal or serious injury to persons within an area of at least 300 feet from the point of explosion. Protective barriers, i.e. walls and vehicles, will lessen the distance required, depending on the size of the bomb. Bystanders should be kept away from the windows, since explosions frequently break glass and have often caused blindness in cases in which spectators watching burning explosives were injured when the fire caused an explosion. If the suspected item weighs less than a pound and has no fragmentation, people may be safe from serious injury in adjoining rooms, depending on the thickness of walls and floors or the location of the bomb within the room. Three hundred feet away is usually safe, except from fragments or bombs over fifty pounds. However, fragments rarely travel more than one thousand feet in a bombing.

The anti-personnel bomb in a vehicle that is loaded with explosives requires a larger evacuation area of approximately two blocks, or six hundred to a thousand feet. Broken windows from city buildings create hazards far beyond similar bombs in rural areas.

Under no circumstances should the police officer or fire fighter touch a suspected bomb or explosive. Suspected bombs or explosives should not be disturbed by persons other than the bomb squad. Simply put, the police should move the people away from the bomb and not move the bomb away from the people. Some explosives are so sensitive they cannot be moved, and some bombs are designed to explode when moved.

Members of the public safety department should establish and maintain police lines at a safe distance until the removal of the suspected item by members of the explosive disposal section. The police officers should be prepared to render first aid if necessary. Also, they should be alert for possible suspects or witnesses. Photographs of bystanders may later reveal the suspect at the scene.

The communications bureau should contact the explosives disposal section immediately upon notification of any type of explosive or explosion case. Some departments require that a rescue squad and/or an ambulance and a fire truck stand by at every location where the bomb squad is involved in disposal work. Training for paramedics and doctors in traumatic bomb injuries is advisable in preparation before these events. Coordination of these units avoids life-threatening delays in communications and transportation.

BOMB SQUAD NOTIFICATION

The member of the explosives disposal section who receives the call should advise communications when a call comes from other than the communications bureau. Immediate response should be provided on any call about explosives, and the bomb disposal vehicle should be taken on every call. The complainant or police officer often incorrectly identifies the suspected item. If the call comes through another individual, the message is often distorted. The bomb technician receiving the call should not advise the caller to move a suspect item, because he cannot tell exactly what it is by another person's description. He should not waste time obtaining information on the telephone that can better be obtained at the scene, especially if the suspect item seems to be a time bomb, because every second may count. The bomb technician should proceed to the scene as rapidly as possible without endangering lives. You may find yourself tensing up and worrying about what you are going to do when you get to the scene because someone has reported an item as a time bomb. Upon inspection, you may find it is not a bomb at all. Just make sure the necessary equipment is kept in repair and is taken with you in case you need it. A bomb disposal technician's life depends upon his knowledge and his ability to use his equipment. He must be thoroughly trained before he arrives at a scene.

ARRIVAL

Upon arrival, the bomb specialist will contact the officer in charge. Often the officers at the scene will greet the bomb technician with, "Boy, we sure are glad to see you." Although they are glad to see him, they do not associate with him too closely when he works on a bomb. The explosive disposal technician will obtain as much information as possible about the case before approaching the suspected object.

Information to be gathered is first, Why do you think it is a bomb? This may sound like a stupid question, but it sure saves time. One police officer at a scene answered the query with, "Because it's got dynamite and a clock and wires to it." There was no need for further talk. The second question may be Where is the bomb? if you do not see it immediately upon your arrival. Other questions that may be helpful are: Has it been moved? Where did it come from? What is it suspected of being? When was it first discovered? Who discovered it? Is there any reason anyone would have for setting the bomb or explosive? The explosive disposal technician may contact officers, fire fighters, detectives, complainants, witnesses or suspects for this information. (Of course, since the Miranda decision, you have to advise a suspect of his rights first.)

ASSISTANCE

Before approaching the bomb, the technician will advise officers or fire fighters at the scene to stand back and to apply first aid if needed. In most cases, only one man is needed to work on a bomb. But if you are injured, you will need someone else to give you first aid. If two people are injured, then one may have to wait for help while the other is treated. If you want someone near you for moral support, you may later feel sorry if they are injured along with you. When I was severely injured in an explosion, I found that I had to give first aid to a less-injured bystander who was temporarily blinded by the bright flash.

Examination

The purpose of an examination of a suspected improvised explosive device, or bomb, is to identify and analyze the item through recognition in order to create a basis for the bomb disposal technician to decide the safest method of disposing the item in question. During this examination, evidence is recorded in the form of visual, olfactory and auditory perception. Through the use of cameras, description, notes, measurements, x-rays, explosive vapor detectors and sound detectors, evidence may be recorded for future investigation and court purposes.

Robots

The United Kingdom developed the first robots and disrupters that were used in the disposal of improvised explosive devices (IED). These developments have dramatically changed the entire approach to bomb disposal problems. However, injuries still occur, mainly because the robot is not used for one of its best purposes: examination of suspected improvised explosive devices. If a suspected IED is reported, there is seldom any need to risk lives of humans or explosive detecting dogs to verify what is a dangerous situation. It is true that every situation is different, but why take extra risks when a machine can do the job?

A robot can examine a suspect IED or bomb visually and record the item with the robot's color video camera. Yet, the use of video recorders attached to the television monitor are infrequently used for this lifesaving and evidence-saving purpose.

The robotic television cameras can permanently record the suspect IED on a VCR, in case it blows up or is torn apart by the disrupter. It can also be used to permanently and remotely x-ray the suspect IED. The author has done this with a prototype, but none of the robot or x-ray manufacturers have developed this as a fixed arrangement. The state of the art, in 1994, is still x-raying with radiographs in very few incidents. This procedure requires the robot to return to the handler to develop the film.

Another improvement which the author has used in practice is the remote examination of a suspect bomb with an electronic explosive vapor detector mounted on a robot. While not as good as a dog, a remotely operated explosive detector does not risk the lives of a dog handler or a dog to examine a suspected item.

Many improvised explosive devices are duds or misfires and will never explode unless they are disturbed. Other varieties of improvised explosive devices are extremely sensitive. A time-initiated bomb may be ready to explode. A suspected improvised explosive device may be a command-initiated bomb. All of these categories of bombs may explode when the bomb technician approaches to examine the item or if the technician moves the item. Otherwise, the item may never explode. Why take unnecessary risks examining a suspected bomb when a robot may do it almost as well or better than a technician?

If anyone advises a bomb technician that an item is a bomb, the technician should believe him until investigation proves otherwise. The examination should take place remotely, if possible. Usually there is no need for a bomb technician to go near a bomb to examine it, if the technician has a robot. Every bomb squad should have a robot. The least expensive robot in 1994 is $14,500. If a bomb disposal technician does not have a robot, then he should make a shield which can be made for approximately $1,000.

Not only can a suspected bomb be examined with a robot, but the robot can be used to search certain areas for a bomb that cannot be easily reached by a bomb technician.

A hand on a robot, as seen in Figure 49, can rotate to insert and turn keys and doorknobs. An additional arm on a robot would be an enormous advantage in some incidents. This second arm, which does not need to be movable, could be used by a robot to hold a suspected bomb in place while the main movable arm and hand open the item in question to determine its contents. There are benefits gained by this action. Evidence may be saved. If the suspected item is not a bomb and is quite valuable, this less violent method of examination results in fewer financial claims and better public relations.

Another advantage of a robot is that it can be used for radiological surveys of suspected bombs or material without endangering a human life by excessive exposure.

Figure 49. The associate members of the International Association of Bomb Technicians and Investigators are manufacturers and distributors of equipment who respond directly to requests and advice of its members for the type of research and development that the technicians want.

METHODS OF DISPOSAL

Command Post

When using a robot, bomb disposal technicians need to set up a command post which is a location where a technician will monitor and control the robot. With some bomb squads, this command post may be a fixed position in the bomb truck or trailer as shown in Figure 50. Some monitors and control panels for robots are large but are easily moved. The bomb technician or robot's operator may wish to have a line of sight on the robot to facilitate orientation with the area. The bomb technician/robot handler should be at the safest and most remote area possible. The bomb technician should be aware of possible secondary bombs which have been secreted in obvious sites where command posts may be set up.

In dangerous areas, where there is the possibility of snipers, a security perimeter may have to be established with armed personnel. Personnel

Figure 50. The state of the art in robot monitoring systems has many features. Among possibilities are the use of the recorder on the right to fluoroscope suspect bombs with a pulse x-ray. The robot does not have to return to develop the x-ray film.

in the security perimeter should be on the alert for possible assassins who may have radio-controlled initiation systems for bombs.

Radio-controlled bombs are becoming more frequent. If it is known what type of control device bombs may use, jamming signals may be transmitted to prematurely explode their bombs in manufacture or delivery. Scene security personnel may spot command bombers in a suspected vicinity, or other suspect items or concealed dual electric wire in the vicinity.

Monitors or control panels for robots may be small enough to permit being hand-carried while operating the robot. Monitors require rechargeable batteries and/or alternating current and/or direct-current power connections. Robots may be both radio controlled and/or through a cable tether. The radio control is much better because the cable is cumbersome. The self-winding light cable, as in Figure 51, is the latest tether design. A wheeled robot, or tracked robot, is a matter of choice for the type of terrain to be encountered.

Figure 51. This new lightweight self-winding cable overcomes a lot of the problems of backing a robot away from a bomb.

Small robots are less expensive and can operate in smaller areas, but in some cases large robots are necessary for larger bombs, longer reach and more equipment. The problem of two-dimension monitoring screens is eased slightly by multiple screens with measuring probes.

The more practice time that a bomb disposal technician has with a robot, the easier it is for him to handle various situations. The technician may have several choices of operation with a suspected bomb during a remote examination of the suspected device. The robot may dismantle the bomb in several ways or move it to another location, including into a bomb carrier.

By far, the safest and most expeditious method of disposal is the use of the disrupter, on or off the robot. The disrupter may be set in place and the robot returned to a safe area before the disrupter is fired remotely. Figure 52 shows a suspected bomb that was opened with a disrupter.

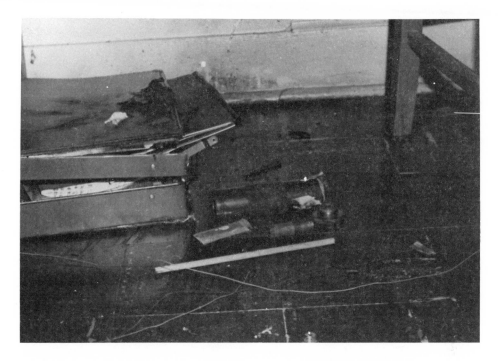

Figure 52. During a bomb scare a briefcase was found that was suspected of being a bomb. The disrupter was used in place with a water bullet as shown in the photograph.

In-Place Detonation

The safest method of disposal of any bomb or explosive is to blow it up in place by setting another charge on it. A robot can carry an explosive charge to the suspected bomb and place the charge, release it, and return to a safe area while the charge is initiated remotely by the bomb disposal technician. The charge can be controlled electrically, electronically or mechanically as seen in Figure 53. The charge should not be initiated with a time-delay fuse unless absolutely necessary. During the delay time, an intruder may unknowingly approach the suspect item. If there is no need to worry about property damage, this is a fine method. Some bombs may require a large amount of explosive shock to explode them. Some thick containers may require a shape charge for penetration.

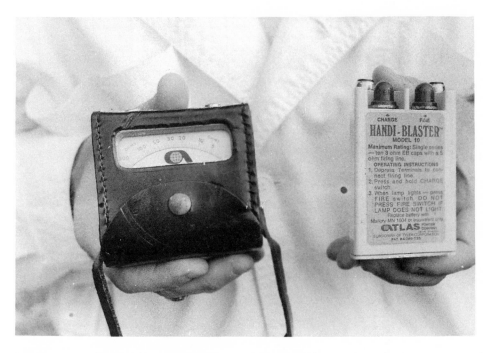

Figure 53. For the safest blasting techniques, circuits should be tested with a galvanometer, and a blasting machine should have sufficient current for the circuit.

Freezing

If cryogenics or freezing is the preferred method of disposal, the bomb technician will carry the equipment with him when he approaches the bomb. This method is not new. Sergeant Cote of Montreal found an article in a Paris magazine depicting this as the safest method back in 1914, according to Monsieur Kling of the Paris City Laboratory, who also described dismantling two anarchists' bombs with the use of an x-ray machine. A camera may be carried to take a "before" picture of the bomb in case it explodes.

Freezing has been a subject of periodic experimentation. The most developed method of freezing is as follows: two technicians approach the items, place a large styrofoam icebox upside down over the bomb without moving it and apply liquid nitrogen through a small hole in the box. Ice is not formed, but batteries, corrosive delays, dynamite, caps and clocks can be made inert in various lengths of time up to thirty minutes. It may take some items less than a minute to be made inactive. While the styrofoam box is being placed and the valve of the nitrogen tank is being opened, the technician can quickly observe the bomb. While the freezing process takes place, the technician retreats from the bomb. After the bomb has been frozen, it is safe to dismantle, since none of the components will function. To facilitate freezing, an entry hole may have to be made into a closed bomb for insertion of the needle nose nozzle of the nitrogen tank hose. This hole may be made remotely by use of a projectile-firing device.

Obviously, this method requires long time exposure on target of not only one technician but two. Thus far, no one has experimented with a robot to attempt to freeze a bomb due to the awkwardness and bulk of the equipment. An independent company cannot afford to spend time and money on research and development of equipment and methods unless a market demands it.

In 1972, the Army gave state-of-the-art cryogenics equipment to the Metro Dade Police Bomb Squad for possible use during the Republican National Convention. The equipment was thoroughly tested and carried on a bomb truck for years, but no one chose to use it on any of the many suspected improvised explosive device cases that occurred during that period. The nitrogen tank had to be refilled every month because it naturally bled off, and it took up specially designed space on the vehicle. Disadvantages of freezing are several. Allegedly while being frozen, the granules and molecules of an explosive may move and grate against each other. Some dangerous chemicals that are more sensitive to shock may be isolated because they do not freeze as fast as others. When nitroglycerine is thawing, it is more sensitive to shock. Two batteries in a battery-powered relay may have the wrong battery freeze first, causing the relay to collapse and the charge to fire. If you are not sure what you are freezing, it may be best not to freeze the bomb. If you do freeze it it can be dismantled instead. An Army EOD team in Washington, D. C., reportedly dismantled two bombs by freezing in 1970.

In its effects, freezing is similar to immersion methods or injection of liquids. No cases have been verified where the methods have been used. Immersion in 10W motor oil will penetrate and stop a clock mechanism. However, one alarm clock was found to be running one hour after immersion of a hoax bomb in water by the complainant. The injection of liquid plaster of fast-hardening glue into a mechanism apparatus may be possible, remotely, with a robot or from behind a shield. If not, the suspected bomb would have to be moved remotely with a line first.

Remote Movement

Before the development of robots and disrupters, moving a suspected bomb by remote control, as taught by the New York Bomb Squad, was one of the safest methods of approach. If a robot is not available or is unable to reach a suspected bomb, or a choice is made not to use a disrupter, this method may be considered. Doctor Muhlberger described this technique in *The Journal of Police Science* in 1937. The bomb technician, wearing a bomb suit, will approach the item, pulling one end of a line and carrying a wire cutter and a knife with him. He will rapidly observe and analyze the bomb as he approaches to determine the method that causes the bomb to explode. An open-type bomb may make this readily apparent, but one should not jump to conclusions or hasty decisions. The obvious initiating device, such as a burned-out fuse or a time bomb, may be in the bomb with an anti-disturbance device set inside the explosive itself as a trap to kill the bomb technician.

The technician should remember that the initiating system is frequently on or near the top or outside of a bomb for several reasons. The bomber may add the initiation system after the assembly of other components, the bomber may have attached a safety to the bomb, or the bomber may not initiate the bomb until he delivers the bomb to the target. This is also true of bombs in storage or transportation as shown in Figure 54.

If the technician is sure the item is a time bomb, he may change his procedure and work rapidly as shown in Figure 55. The author dismantled three corrosive delay firing device bombs that had been delivered to their targets. Time pencils were also reported to be used in New York City by Cuban exiles and once in California by revolutionaries. The bomber usually leaves the pencil protruding from the bomb where he can reach it to set it. If the time pencil is visible, it can be deactivated by inserting a safety pin through the inspection holes, being careful not to touch the bomb or pencil first. The pin from a police badge or the filler from a ball-point pen works very well. It is not a recommended action to deactivate a time pencil, since the wire may be so weakened it may be broken by any disturbance. If there is no anti-disturbance device, the pencil can be removed from the base explosive and the cap removed from the pencil.

Electric wire connections can be broken by a line pulled remotely instead of by cutting (Fig. 56). Breaking a wire remotely is more likely to

Figure 54. This is one of four improvised sea mines that was recovered from a Cuban terrorist organization. The author dismantled them easily because the initiating system was under the top lid and the dynamite in the bag was in the bottom of the mine.

explode a bomb, but it is safer for the technician because one of the main causes of misfires in electrical systems is bad contacts, and any disturbance may make a better contact, causing the bomb to explode. Cutting the wrong wire in a battery-powered relay collapsing circuit (battery decay circuit) may cause the bomb to explode. Whatever procedure is used, the technician must be careful not to move the wire when cutting it, attaching a line or contacting two wires at a time. It is difficult to cut a wire with wire cutters and have both jaws of the cutter touch the wire at the same time so that it is not moved. Small wire cutters are better for insertion between parts of a bomb than linemen's pliers. In Puerto Rico, in 1968, a bomb squad detective was critically injured while trying to insert a wire cutter between a watch and explosive to cut a wire. Fortunately, the police officer lived because of quick thinking, but his health has been affected ever since.

The type of line preferred for moving a bomb remotely may be a quarter-inch rope, since it may not slip under a bomb as string does when a loose loop of line is laid around the bomb without touching it

Figure 55. The author quickly broke the tape holding the time pencil in this container of C4 and removed the time pencil as well as the cap from the time pencil.

(Fig. 57). Then from behind a barrier, the line is pulled to jar the bomb to determine if it has an anti-disturbance device. A grappling hook may be thrown over a bomb or placed on the ground and the technician walks in a semicircle around the bomb to the other side. The hook is then dragged across the bomb to move it remotely without the technician's actually getting near it, but sometimes this does not catch (Fig. 58).

One of the benefits of a robot is that a bomb technician does not have to be concerned with the urgency of time as he does when he has to approach a suspected bomb in person. Time bombs make it necessary for a bomb technician to reach the scene of a suspected bomb as quickly as possible before it explodes, or to await certain time delays.

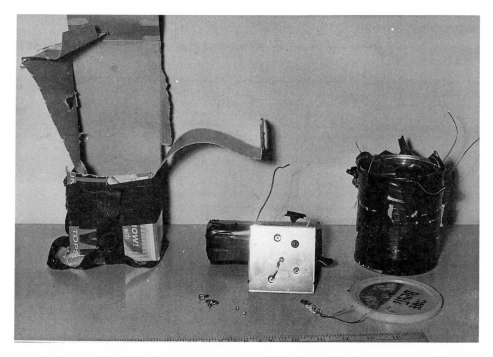

Figure 56. A time bomb in West Palm Beach that was moved and deactivated by the author with a ¼-inch rope. This technique was used successfully twice on partly open bombs, because exposed wiring presented the opportunity and we did not have a robot.

Hook and Line

Placing a hook with a line attached to it, on a suspected bomb, is one of the most dangerous acts that a person can do. It is not recommended but is related in the event there is no other method possible. A disrupter on a robot is, or a disrupter is, the safest method of dealing with most bombs. The author used this method several times on suspect bombs and actual bombs before robots and disrupters were developed.

Dismantling or remote moving of suspected bombs has been developed to a fine science by Norman Lier and others at the Hazardous Devices School at Redstone Arsenal. Through the years technicians have developed ingenious methods of remotely moving suspect bombs in practice and in actual situations. The problems are that these methods usually take time and are more likely to cause a suspect bomb to explode. Using a disrupter, a technician may approach a suspect item only once. When a hook or tape is used, lines may occasionally snag or slip. Once a suspect item is

Figure 57. Two Cuban fighter planes at the Miami International Airport exploded and two bombs were found in the engine compartments of other aircraft. Two more bombs were found in a paper bag in nearby weeds.

Figure 58. The author was unable to attach a line to the two bombs still in the other aircraft, so he lifted the bombs out and dismantled the bombs by cutting the fuse and removing the caps. This was before the invention of disrupters and robots. Note the burned fuse and fuse residue before the bomb was removed.

moved, it may become more sensitive unless the initiation system of the suspect item has been interrupted.

By the use of monofilament-reinforced tape and a self-releasing snatch block as shown in Figure 59, suspect bombs can be moved from where they are found. This includes around corners and other barriers, through doors and windows to an area where a disrupter may be used, or the suspect item placed in a carrier for disposal elsewhere. The entire procedure is done usually to save property, but this method causes risks to bomb technicians and is more likely to cause a suspect item to explode instead of using a disrupter and robot to dismantle the suspect device.

Figure 59. Rigging such as shown in this photograph can be utilized to remotely move suspect bombs around, under, over or through obstacles to a disposal area. The safest method is to disrupt suspect bombs in place.

X-Ray

An x-ray machine with a fluoroscope screen is very helpful for possible determination of whether or not an item is a bomb. Doctor Muhlberger described a package bomb which he dismantled by the use of an x-ray machine in 1937. After the suspected bomb has been moved, it can be placed in front of the x-ray tube (Fig. 60). The portable x-ray tube can be placed on the ground approximately one to two feet from the item. The fluoroscope screen can be placed on the ground or hand held on the other side of the item as close to the item as possible for sharpest detail. If the fluoroscope screen is held a greater distance from the item, it magnifies the item but causes it to lose its clarity. The enlarged silhouette is usually not helpful to the technician. A complete view of the item is limited by the size of the fluoroscope screen.

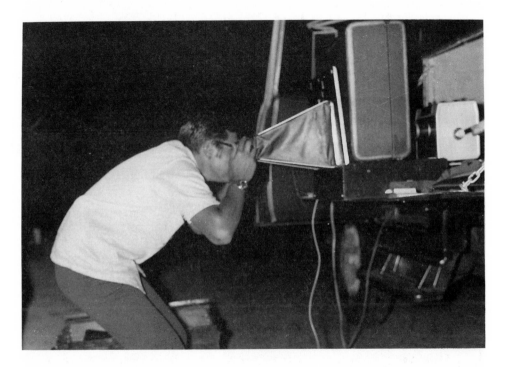

Figure 60. Following Doctor Muhlberger's techniques, suspect bombs can be fluoroscoped with the x-ray machine and a lead-lined screen.

The x-ray machine should be used on lowest voltage and milliamperage to lessen the amount of radiation to the operator and also because this is usually sufficient to visualize the contents of most containers. The operator should wear a film badge when using the machine. X-ray damage is cumulative in the body, and a film badge service will advise you if you have too much exposure, although this hardly ever happens if the machine is used with discretion. The lead-lined attache case and fluoroscope screen make the operation easier on the operator than holding a hand screen with lead gloves and apron (Fig. 61). Bright light will make viewing difficult if there is not a tight seal between the face and the fluoroscope screen. If the intensity of the x-ray is increased, heavier containers may be penetrated.

If the container is too thick, a radiograph will be needed. Ordinary black-and-white film in a 4 × 5-inch film holder can be used for radiographs; however, a polaroid x-ray film developer has several advantages: (a) an object too thick for fluoroscoping can be examined internally by a long time exposure on film; (b) a picture provides a permanent record in the event the item explodes; (c) time spent near a bomb fluoroscoping it may be shortened since the film may be developed and studied at a safe distance; (d) radiation exposure for the technician is less; and (e) a television camera has been developed to use with the x-ray machine so the operator will not be in danger if the bomb has been rigged to explode by x-ray. This is expensive and may be too much for any budget unless the sky is the limit. The price is approximately $10,000.

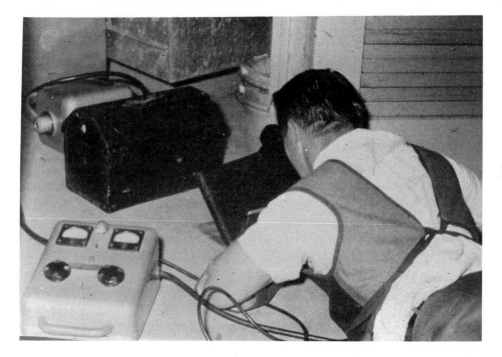

Figure 61. The author is using lead and rubber gloves and apron to fluoroscope a suspected satchel in the Miami Police property room. This technique only requires one approach to a suspect bomb that has been handled.

Pulse x-ray machines are less expensive and are battery-powered. Figure 62 illustrates one of the most commonly used pulse x-rays. Now they are able to be viewed with television screens and video recorders as shown in Figure 63.

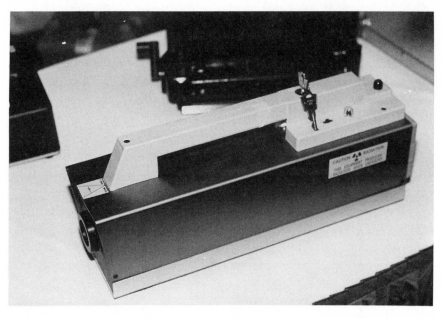

Figure 62. Pulse x-ray machines have improved so that they are approximately half the size of a loaf of bread.

Remote Opening

An enclosed bomb can be opened remotely by several methods. The safest method is by use of a robot which offers a variety of procedures. Part of the examination of a suspect enclosed bomb is examination, as in medical terms intrusive or non-intrusive. A suspect item may be moved by a robot to a bomb carrier or other location. A robot may use a firearm or disrupter fired from the robot arm. A firearm or disrupter may be left by the robot in firing position, and the robot retreats to a safe area before initiation of the remote opening method.

The British developed the first disrupter and have used their "pig-stick" successfully to dismantle many actual bombs. Bomb technicians throughout the world owe their lives to the British for the development of the disrupter.

Figure 63. A pulse x-ray can now be viewed on video screens without having to bring a film cassette back to be developed.

Many Americans copied the United States Armed Forces shotgun de-armer, as shown in Figure 64, and followed the British method of water propelled at high speed to disrupt bombs. Various means of initiation, propellant loads and mediums, e.g. sand, plaster, pulverized steel or slugs, are used depending on individual situations and choice.

The Canadian disrupter is their state of the art and it can be used with laser sighting so a robot or person may not have to approach a suspect bomb too closely. This disrupter, as illustrated in Figure 65, has been on the market and used successfully for years.

The American disrupter is the latest development of the Federal Bureau of Investigation at Sandia Laboratory. Chris Cherry directed many successful tests in opening pipe bombs which contained sensitive initiating systems or sensitive explosives. The disrupter is shown in Figure 66. The purpose is to open and deactivate suspect bombs with the least chance of causing them to explode. Low cost and ease of use make this tool available for almost any department or manufacturer to duplicate.

In the forties, before the invention of robots and disrupters, the New York City Bomb Squad developed the use of bomb tongs. This was one of the best methods of opening suspect closed bombs before 1972. The tongs

Figure 64. Shotgun dearmers had been in use for many years by the military. The British developed the idea of using it with water to disrupt suspected improvised explosive devices. Different types of steel slugs or avon rounds are used to disrupt suspected pipe bombs.

were used after a suspect item had been moved remotely and x-rayed. The author successfully used this method (shown in Figure 67) on many suspect improvised explosive devices before disrupters became available. The main problems with this method are spending too much time near the suspect item, the possibility of the tongs slipping and rough handling. The bomb tongs are simply two pairs of large ice tongs with extra teeth welded to each jaw, so that there are three sharp teeth to grip a container. If the teeth slip, a piece of adhesive tape can be placed on the side of the container for the teeth to bite into. Once the teeth grip a package, the harder the pull, the harder they bite. A chain and ring are welded across the handles of each pair of tongs, to which a heavy rope is attached. One rope is tied to a heavy post or fixed object. The other rope is tied to the rear of the bomb truck. This rope is longer, of course, in case there should be an explosion.

Firing projectiles at a bomb can be done with .38's or rifles from a distance, but unless the container is opened completely, this method may make the bomb more dangerous.

Figure 65. The laser sighting system on this disrupter makes it possible to reach suspected bombs in high or remote areas. The bomb disposal technician or robot may set up the disrupter 20 feet distance from a bomb.

A shotgun placed near the bomb, held in place with sandbags, and the trigger pulled with string will make larger holes in the container, but, unless well aimed, it may take several shots (Fig. 68). A Garand rifle also fired by string tied to the trigger with a dummy rifle grenade attached is more effective. This will smash open most fiber or wood-trim suitcases or metal suitcases. An empty flare grenade with the flare removed and a coffee can welded to it will make a hole through a fiberboard suitcase the same size as the coffee can, not unlike a cookie cutter. This provides a good interior view and enough space to insert a hand if necessary. A 37-mm teargas gun can be fired remotely with similar results.

Blasting caps taped to locks or latches of suitcases will usually remove the mechanism without too-extensive damage to the suitcase and contents as used in Figures 69 and 70.

A great deal of experimentation and practical use by different bomb squads, government agencies and private companies have resulted in numerous ways of using remote methods in dealing with suspected

Figure 66. The United States Department of Justice developed this disrupter which dismantles bombs with the least probability of causing them to explode.

bombs. Platter charges, or flying discs of metal that are propelled with explosives, may be used against hard container bombs. An advantage of this type of entry, or dismantling procedure, is that the technician may not have to approach the suspect item closely, in some instances because the explosive tool may be aimed from a distance. A disadvantage is that the flying piece of metal may travel long distances.

Plastic bowls, filled with water, or other soft mediums, may be propelled with explosives, in the same manner, to dismantle or remotely open suspect bombs.

Other remote opening methods include small amounts of detonating cord or primers. Vehicles, that may possibly contain bombs, may be opened by this method. Envelopes or small packages can be opened by remotely initiating small explosive charges close to the suspect item. A white envelope, containing the plastic explosive in Figure 71, had the bomber's fingerprints on it.

Acid trepanning is a simple, time-consuming method of entering steel containers without initiating anti-disturbance devices. One method of removing bulk explosives from a bomb is by steaming. Although the

Figure 67. Thanks to the research and development of robots and disrupters, this technique of using tongs to pull suspect bombs apart is no longer necessary.

British used this method in World War II, and trepanning equipment is inexpensive, very few bomb squads obtain this equipment or train in its use. Some situations may require such a procedure.

Some of the explosive remote opening techniques for suspect bombs have been adopted for rapid entry into buildings for hostage rescue operations. Doors, windows, walls, roofs and floors may be breeched in emergencies, with minimum amounts of explosives or propellants. The Ester recoilless disrupter can be handled as shown in Figure 72 or initiated remotely.

Shields

Dismantling bombs remotely with a protective shield and long extended poles fitted with tools will provide some safety to the operator. Disadvantages are the limited visibility and control in critical work and the time

Figure 68. The use of firearms to dismantle bombs was one of the few options years ago that had erratic consequences when trying to deactivate bombs.

spent setting up the shield. The advantage of this method is distance. A high-velocity explosion will have a central shattering point that disintegrates everything within the area. The damaging effects from explosions are heat, pressure and fragmentation. Depending on the type of bomb and the type of target, one of the three may do more damage than the others. The central shattering effect is pressure, and the amount of pressure falls off rapidly in inversely square proportion to the distance. Thus a little distance may make you a lot safer. A pressure wave striking a shield will push against it. If the shield is V-shaped, the blast will deflect off it at an angle. If the shield is round, it will offer more resistance. Toronto and Los Angeles have shields made of two layers of aluminum separated by wood. Experimentation with a fiberglass shield has shown even better performance.

A good example of this phenomenon of shielding is that used by stuntmen in daredevil shows. The showman will get into a cardboard or wooden box, coffin or house and detonate dynamite, completely shattering the container. In the smoke afterward, he pushes down the shield that the audience does not see. The point of a quarter-inch steel shield is eight

Figure 69. Before disrupters and robots, the author taped blasting caps to this suspected bomb found at the Miami International Airport.

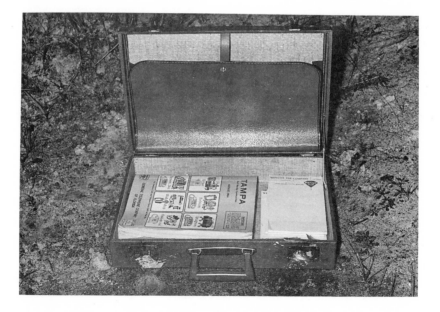

Figure 70. Caps taped to the latches of briefcases usually was a successful method of opening them, but it required proximity of the suspect bomb and touching it.

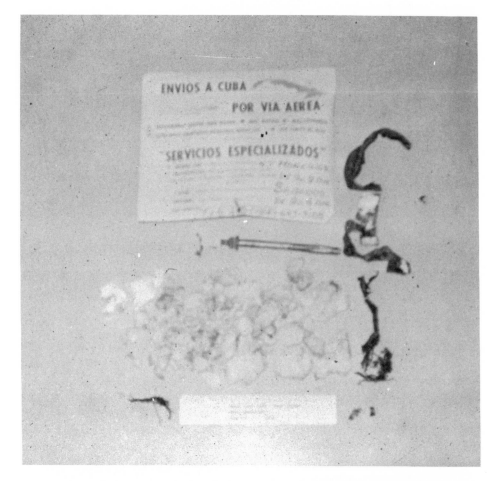

Figure 71. Shown in this photograph are four ounces of C4 that had been in an envelope and which was scattered by the cap that was on the time pencil. Another bomb that was initiated by the burned fuse and a cap caused the misfire. Always look for a second bomb at scenes of bombs and bombings.

inches away from the side of six sticks of dynamite. The shield is two feet high and held at a 90-degree angle or 45-degree angle from the dynamite. The shield is angled for two feet, and sides are parallel to the daredevil. He wears a football helmet which covers his ears, and he exhales prior to the explosion.

The shield and equipment used by Toronto are described by D. D. Lucas in the *Canadian Journal of Forensic Sciences.*

The Metro Dade Police copied the Canadian shield and used it with great success as shown in Figure 73. The author used the shield on twenty-five suspect bomb cases and was the first known person to actually

Figure 72. This powerful disrupter developed by Gerd Ester can be initiated remotely on suspect bombs or used in series or hand held for rapid entry.

dismantle a bomb from behind a shield. The bomb consisted of 7.5 pounds of dynamite with a radio control and was located under the car seat. Other members of the Metro Dade Police Bomb Squad also used the shield. John Murray, one of my replacements in the bomb squad, used the shield to remove a bomb from a mailbox that a robot could not reach.

A shield is referred to as a sled by some technicians. Two, or more, instructors at the Hazardous Devices School have tested a shield by remaining behind it while exploding ten pounds of dynamite ten feet in front of the shield. The shield has a lexan window and is made of titanium, which is the strongest and lightest known metal. The fiberglass poles fit through holes in the shield. John Lurvey, a former partner of the author, placed the flaps over the poles as added protection. A bomb

Figure 73. This photograph was taken of the author dismantling a suspect bomb at a post office. This technique is more dangerous but preserves more evidence or valuable items than the disrupters which are now used.

technician in Venezuela lost a hand, because at the moment of the explosion his hand was above the shield, manipulating a pole while dismantling a pipe bomb.

Before a robot was purchased, the shield was transported on the bomb truck, as shown in Figure 74. The cost of the shield was approximately $1,800. Construction was by the Metro Dade Public Works Motor Pool. The adjustable tools and poles are supplied by electric power equipment manufacturers. The poles do not conduct electricity and in an explosion will disintegrate into harmless shreds. Additional tools are a two-inch-wide machete blade, which is doubled-edged serrated on both edges, a Lurvey Bomb Grabber, as shown in Figure 75, and a dog snare.

With less expensive shield material and foot power, the shield can be built for less than $1,000. The shield is a poor man's robot. If a bomb squad is unable to obtain a robot, a shield may be personally financed, since it is a lifesaving tool. It is an improvement over a bomb suit because

Figure 74. From behind the shield a suspect bomb may be dismantled or moved to another location. A disrupter may be placed near a suspect item from behind the shield.

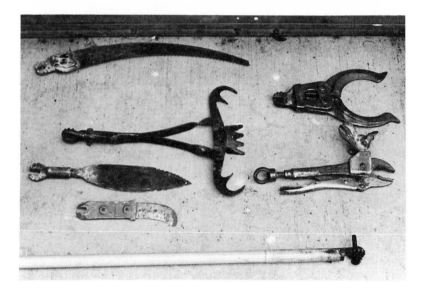

Figure 75. The most commonly used tools with the shield were the hook knife, the double-edged serrated knife and the Lurvey bomb grabber. A little practice is all a technician needs to become proficient with these distance-creating tools.

the bomb technician is further away from the bomb. The technician's hands are not exposed to direct contact with a suspect bomb. Canadian experiments have shown that the effects are many times more dangerous within three feet of the center of an explosion than eight feet away.

The sixteen-foot poles are extended eight feet from the shield and make a good balancing fulcrum to facilitate handling of the tools. An advantage over the robot is that the shield allows the technician to have two remote arms instead of only one. This feature allows the technician to dismantle many suspect items that would be destroyed by a disrupter. Not only does the shield save evidence in this manner, but it also permits the technician to save expensive items that may be in a suspect object that is not a bomb. Bomb squads must be aware of criticism that they blow up anything that is even remotely suspicious, as the next time something suspicious is found, the bomb squad may not be called and people will take unnecessary risks with suspect items. Less violent methods of opening suspect bombs may be advisable in some situations.

A bomb that is dismantled from behind the shield is more likely to explode than if a disrupter is used. A disrupter can be delivered to a suspect bomb by a technician from behind the shield, and then retreat with the shield to a safe area to initiate the disrupter.

The most commonly used tools with the shield were a hook knife to hold suspect bombs down while using the double-serrated machete blade, or spear, to rip items apart. With these tools and a little practice, a technician is able to cut open envelopes, bags, suitcases and boxes, to push buttons and flip latches on brief cases.

Light suspect bombs can be carried, dragged or pulled to other locations including a bomb carrier.

Mitigation

The act of placing a bomb blanket over a suspect bomb may initiate the bomb by moving it or applying pressure on it. A timing device may initiate the bomb, while the person placing the blanket is near the bomb or it is initiated by command. Standoff spacers around the bomb, consisting of a ring of cardboard or kevlar, help offset the problem of movement or pressure initiating a bomb; setting spacers increases the time that a person may be near a bomb but may make a blanket more effective in catching fragments.

A blanket may make a bomb technician's job more difficult because he may have to deal with the removal of the blanket which may initiate a bomb. About the only time a bomb blanket may be used is when it may be worth the risk of life to insulate a suspect bomb because a bomb disposal technician may be delayed.

Other forms of mitigation of bomb effects are foam or water. In situations where barriers can be set up or barriers exist to hold foam in place, it can cover a suspect bomb before a disrupter or other means of disposal is attempted.

If water is used, there must be sufficient space for the water to escape or move during the explosion. Otherwise, the water will only add to the effects of the explosion. Water will not only help slow down fragments but will mainly diminish heat and dissipate pressure. Recent testing with a half-gallon cardboard container wrapped with tape and stacked a short distance from a bomb have proven to be quite successful. The increased use of water surrounding explosives helped to expedite the extinguishing of oil well fires in Kuwait after the Gulf War.

Necessity led to the development of Bomb Bags by a South African. The bags are filled with water and can be thrown or placed over grenades, Molotov cocktails, pipe bombs or other small bombs if there is not sufficient time to leave the area of a bomb before it explodes. Figure 76 depicts a bomb bag.

Another recent type of mitigation is the hanging of plastic bags of water on vertical surfaces before an explosion to protect the surface and attenuate damaging effects in front of and behind the surface.

Use of Body Armor

In the first edition of *Bombs and Bombings* the author cited the need for improvement of body armor. Through expensive research and development many improvements have been made. Bomb suits have been tested against pressure, heat and fragmentation. Many changes have resulted in increased protection against these effects and concussion from impact with the ground. The new suits are easier and faster to put on or take off. The MedEng suit from Canada, as shown in Figure 77, is the state-of-the-art suit and helmet. A spine-reinforcement feature not only adds protection to the backbone but also helps make the suit more comfortable.

A light cooling suit under the bomb suit increases the time that a technician can work in the suit. A communications system and a face shielding improve protection and visibility. Increased flexibility of the suit has been obtained to offset the feeling of claustrophobia for the wearer. Several companies blew up a lot of suits to gather input from

Figure 76. Water can lessen the effects of a bomb considerably, but there must be sufficient room for the water to dissipate or it may create additional damage. More experimentation and information are necessary.

bomb technicians, throughout the world, in bringing about these lifesaving improvements.

Videotapes of tests have helped convince bomb technicians to wear bomb suits that have saved the lives of several technicians who have been blown up.

Transportation

Transportation of a suspect bomb or a sensitive explosive requires many decisions. Will the item possibly explode? Will more people and property be endangered by movement? Is it safer to dismantle or deactivate the item in place? How much of a commotion or spectacle will be created by the transportation of the item? Is it best done with a marked or unmarked vehicle?

Even though the author is one of the inventors of the most common bomb carrier, the top-vented container, it is seldom used in Dade County.

Figure 77. Expensive research and development and input from bomb technicians have helped industry produce safer, more flexible and more comfortable bomb suits.

Disrupters and/or robots make transportation of suspect bombs a less viable choice of methods to deal with a problem. Figure 78 shows the author placing old dynamite in the first Brodie-Dykes-Zmuda bomb carrier.

Figure 78. The best method of dealing with bombs is to disrupt them in place. Some sensitive explosives are best loaded remotely into a bomb carrier for disposal elsewhere.

Storage

Storage of explosives or bombs is necessary for preservation of evidence. Two magazines should be provided, one for blasting caps and firing devices and one for bulk explosives (Fig. 79). These should be located in areas that are secure from theft and away from inhabited buildings. Dirt embankments surrounding the magazines will direct blast waves upwards in the event of an accidental explosion. Some homemade chemical explosives, leaky dynamite, badly corroded caps or ordnance may not be stable and should be taken to the blasting range for immediate disposal.

A third magazine may be necessary for storage of fireworks. Fireworks may be especially sensitive to friction and may ignite or explode with

Figure 79. Safe storage of explosives requires dirt embankments to direct the force of possible accidental explosions upwards. Only compatible explosives should be stored in the same magazines.

movement or spontaneous combustion. Ammonium nitrate or sodium nitrate are found in commercial explosives, i.e. dynamite, emulsions, nitro carbo nitrate or other blasting agents. According to Volume Three of *Urbanski's Encyclopedia of Explosives,* ammonium nitrate or sodium nitrate should not be stored with chlorates. Chlorates are found in fireworks. If the two are stored together, or there is a saturation of the floor of a storage magazine of previous chemicals, ammonium chlorate may form. Ammonium chlorate is hypergolic. Some disastrous fires and explosions have occurred in recent years in which bomb disposal technicians have been killed and storage magazines and bomb trucks destroyed. These accidents may happen during handling or storage.

Naval float flares that have misfired should never be stored in a magazine, because they are liable to activate while drying or if they are immersed in water again. They should be disposed of in place or carefully transported to a disposal range and destroyed.

Magazine construction should comply with local, state and federal laws as well as with environmental regulations. Security measures may include alarms, locks, gates and video surveillance. Earth embankments present problems of maintaining vegetation growth in the area. Magazine sites and the location of the bomb disposal ranges are not published for obvious safety factors.

Accurate inventories of all explosives and explosive evidence should be maintained. Bomb disposal technicians may wish to record all blasting they do for future reference, court purposes, inventory or for future inquiries.

Bomb Disposal Range

The site for a bomb disposal range may be a difficult place to obtain. Local, state or federal agencies may have remote tracts of land that are centrally located in a bomb squad's jurisdiction. A cooperative effort with a public works right-of-way property management and a legal adviser may all have to work in conjunction with the local environmental agency for a proper bomb range. Private land is available at local excavation or mining operations, but may require the signing of waivers. The amount of explosives in one explosion, or range limit, may lessen blasting complaints from neighbors.

The range should be a secure area that limits access to people and livestock. The area should be free of excess vegetation to prevent forest fires or brushfires. The ground should be firm enough to permit fire trucks and ambulances. Some departments require that fire and rescue personnel stand by during every bomb range operation. Just as the one-man approach is desired at a suspected bomb site, the same practice should be followed at the bomb range. Only one man should be downrange near a suspect bomb, if it is necessary for anyone to be there.

A blockhouse with bullet-resistant windows, for observing and photographing downrange explosions, is advisable. A buried dual-blasting wire from the blockhouse to downrange is an added convenience that saves considerable time. A recently developed radio-controlled initiator is shown in Figure 80.

Figure 80. Several safe and reliable radio-controlled transmitters and receivers are on the market which are made for commercial and military blasting with coded signals.

METHOD OF DESTRUCTION

At the disposal range, the bomb technician may use a disrupter, or any other means which were described previously, to open or dismantle a suspect bomb. If the bomb is exploded in the bomb carrier, a bomb blanket may be placed over the top of the carrier, or container, to help catch fragments.

At the disposal area, the bomb technician may place a small explosive charge on the item in the container or he may remove the object from the container and open it by remote control, tongs, hooks or with explosives. If large amounts of explosives are shot into the container, this may cause it to weaken. The choice of the type of explosive used for disposal depends upon the hardness of the covering of the bomb, how large a hole is desired in the covering, the sensitivity of the bomb to shock and heat and the desire to retain evidence (Fig. 81). One or more blasting caps may be used. A round-shaped charge may cut the preferred type of hole in the bomb. The explosion can also detonate any explosive in the bomb, which is the safest method for disposal. Although this method may destroy valuable evidence, the evidential value is not worth a loss of life.

Figure 81. Blasting kits may contain det cord, C4, dual wire, shape charges, cap crimper, galvanometer, blasting machine, punch, electric caps, fuse caps and fuse. C4 and det cord are stored separately from the caps.

If the bomb is believed to contain liquid or if you want to save pieces of the item which may not be explosive, the bomb should be placed in a can or container if it is to be opened with explosives. The smallest possible amount of explosives should be used so that the can will hold some of the liquid or pieces for analysis or comparison in case it does not explode. If the charge is placed on top of the suspected item, the contents will not be scattered as widely as by a charge placed under the item (Fig. 82). The area should be searched thoroughly after the explosion to collect the pieces for evidence and to find explosives that failed to detonate completely.

All objects in question should be photographed both in black and white and in color, measured and described as to color and markings before disposal or after, as the safest case may be. All explosions and craters should be photographed for proof that an explosion took place and evidence of the type of explosion it was (Figs. 83, 84, 85 and 86).

Figure 82. The author is shown demonstrating the plasticity and consistency of a block of C4 plastic explosive. It is similar to white play dough or clay.

Unless there is an electrical storm in the vicinity, electric blasting is the most desirable type in most cases because it permits control of the exact time of the blast for photographic purposes. All blasting must be performed by at least two persons.

Procedure

The procedure for testing the blasting circuit and preparing the blast is as follows. One technician should work the safe end of the wire, and one should work the explosive end and prepare the explosive. The man at the explosive end must keep the blasting generator and galvanometer with him at all times. The signal given by the blaster is to spread his arms apart. The technician at the other end of the wire should open the wires and then repeat the signal. The wire must first be tested by the technician's opening it at both ends and applying the galvanometer.

Figure 83. Some of Cuban Power's explosives found in a warehouse. Since most judges correctly believe that explosives would not be safe in a courtroom, a photograph of the explosives may be introduced into evidence. Some courts rule that the defense's expert should be able to examine and test the evidence, but there are reasonable limits.

Figure 84. A bomb is shown that is set to explode. This is a sealed plastic sandwich box filled with crushed pentolite with det cord, a cap and fuse attached. The before and after photographs should be taken at right angles to the ruler and from the same position.

There should be a zero galvanometer reading, indicating there are no short circuits in the wire (a wire broken and penetrating the insulation to touch the other wire).

Figure 85. Photographic proof of the explosion for court, if necessary. A demonstration can be offered for the court and jury, but defense attorneys never accept the offers.

Figure 86. The court-qualified expert would testify that this was an explosive and that it did explode upon initiation.

Next, the blaster should signal with arms crossed. The partner at the safe end splices the wires together and the blaster makes the galvanometer reading. If the needle moves, it indicates a complete circuit. A waving of the arms indicates that the line is ready for use and the partner may leave the wires spliced and approach the explosive end to assist the blaster.

The blasting cap is removed from its accordion fold by holding the cap in one hand and looping the wire next to the cap around one's finger tightly to prevent the cap from slipping from the hand. Next, the wire is straightened by simply dropping the shunted end and then sliding the other hand along the wire from the cap to the shunted end. The cap is put into a hole made by inserting a finger into the ground a safe distance away from other explosives. The blaster turns his back on the cap and removes the shunt on the cap wires. He tests the circuit with the galvanometer, and if he obtains a reading, connects the cap to the blasting wire by splicing and taping the wires securely to make sure they do not short out (this would result in a misfire). In case there is a current, only the cap will explode. The cap is then inserted into the explosive. The blaster retreats to the protective barricade, tests the complete circuit with the galvanometer and connects the blasting generator into the circuit. His partner should set up his camera in the blockhouse behind the bullet-resistant window. The blaster yells "Fire in the hole," three times and fires on a count of three so that his partner can photograph the blast. Another scaled photograph should be taken of the crater left by the explosion.

SUSPECTED BOMB OR IMPROVISED EXPLOSIVE DEVICE CHECKLIST PROCEDURE

The following steps are intended as a procedural guide and will vary with the individual situation.

Preparation Before Receiving Calls:

1. Equipment must be ready to go in bomb vehicle or on a designated shelf in a ready room.
2. All bomb disposal technicians should be thoroughly trained in the use of all equipment.

Receiving Call

1. Obtain correct location and description of item.
2. Advise caller that the item should not be handled or moved and advise evacuation of people from vicinity of bomb.
3. Notify the communications bureau which notifies rescue and fire personnel and other prescribed agencies.
4. Give immediate response to all calls.
5. Take bomb truck on all calls.
6. Do not drive to scene in a hazardous manner.

Upon Arrival

1. Park bomb vehicle at a safe but convenient distance from a suspect bomb.
2. Note arrival time.
3. Contact officer or complainant for information on suspect bomb.
4. Advise officers, fire and rescue personnel or complainant if further evacuation and police lines are necessary.
5. Assistant uncoils rope and fetches tools.
6. Assistant takes distance photographs.
7. Assistant stays at safe distance, prepared to render first aid and transportation to hospital in case of injury.

Robot

1. Assistant opens bomb vehicle and extends ramp.
2. Bomb disposal technician turns robot on and checks all controls and makes sure robot has all necessary equipment on it for the mission.
3. Assistant makes sure area is kept clear without interference for bomb disposal technician or robot.
4. Assistant takes distance photographs and photographs bystanders.
5. Bomb disposal technician directs robot to suspect bomb to examine it and record it with video recorder on television monitor.
6. Bomb disposal technician may use listening device to detect sound.
7. Technician may use vapor detector to examine suspect item for explosives.
8. Technician may use x-ray with fluoroscope and television camera and VCR to examine and permanently record contents of suspected bomb.

9. Technician may aim and fire disrupter from robot.
10. Technician may place and aim disrupter, remove robot to safe area and fire disrupter.
11. Technician may fire robot's shotgun repeatedly at suspect item.
12. Technician may place demolition charge on suspect bomb, remove robot to safe area and initiate the charge from a safe distance.
13. Robot may pick up and carry suspect item to a bomb carrier and place item in carrier.

Disrupter

1. Technician loads disrupter with medium of his choice: water, sand, slug, etc., with propelling round of his choice.
2. Assistant keeps area clear from interference and advises further clearance if necessary.
3. Technician either wires up contacts on disrupter and then carries disrupter to proximity of suspect IED or wires up contacts after placing and aiming disrupter.
4. Technician retreats to safe distance.
5. Technician makes sure area is clear.
6. Technician advises, "Fire in the hole."
7. Technician initiates disrupter.
8. Assistant photographs disrupter action.
9. Technician examines scene.
10. Evidence is collected.

Bomb Suit*

1. Put on cooling suit.
2. Assistant helps bomb technician put on bomb suit.
3. Put on helmet.
4. Check communications on suit.
5. Assistant provides necessary tools, equipment and makes certain no one interferes.
6. Bomb technician advises assistant of his observations and every intended action.
7. Assistant records all communications, if necessary.
8. Bomb technician spends minimum time near bomb and retreats to safe distance.

---

*To be used only if a robot is not available or the robot is not able to reach the suspect bomb.

Type of bomb

Time Bomb

1. If the type of short-time timer is known, the bomb technician may wish to wait a given amount of time.
2. Otherwise, the bomb technician may wish to approach the bomb before time runs out, in an attempt to prevent the bomb from exploding.
3. If there is no other choice, the bomb technician quickly puts on a suit and approaches the item.

Time Pencil

1. Insert pin without touching anything.
2. Remove pencil from explosive.
3. Move away from explosive.
4. Remove cap from pencil by wiggling if it is loose and can come off easily without causing an explosion.

Open Clock and Battery Bomb

1. Cut positive lead wire to cap.
2. Cut negative lead wire to cap.
3. Remove cap from explosive.

Cryogenics

1. Place styrofoam box over bomb.
2. Insert nozzle of hose into styrofoam box.
3. Turn valve and retreat to safe position.
4. Return to bomb after safe time.
5. Turn off valve.
6. Remove box.
7. Dismantle bomb.

Anti-Disturbance-Line Movement

1. Carry one end of line to bomb.
2. Place loop of line around bomb without touching.
3. Retreat to safe position.
4. Make sure everyone is clear.
5. Pull line easy.
6. Jerk line hard.

7. If the suspect bomb is partly open, then a line or hook may be placed on an exposed wire leading to a cap or battery. This may be accomplished only if the wire is not moved.
8. The line is pulled by hard, fast jerks to break the wire or to pull the suspect bomb apart.
9. Any wire pulled loose must not be allowed to move again.
10. In rare instances it may be possible to tie two lines to a suspect bomb that has protruding wires and pull it apart remotely.

Anti-Disturbance-Hook Movement (By Placing)

1. Carry one end of line with hook to desired position near bomb.
2. Walk around bomb in semicircle, 180 degrees across bomb from hook.
3. Drag line across bomb until it hooks bomb and moves it.

Anti-Disturbance-Hook Movement (By Throwing)

1. Throw hook past bomb.
2. Retreat to safe position.
3. Drag line across bomb until it hooks bomb and moves it.

Remote Wire Cutter

1. A wire cutter is placed on the wire without moving it.
2. The wire cutter is initiated from a safe distance.
3. Upon returning to the suspect item, the technician must make sure that the wire is severed and that the severed wire does not complete a circuit.

Portable X-Ray Machine

1. Set x-ray tube facing bomb.
2. Place lead shielding and fluoroscope screen in front of bomb.
3. Turn on machine to minimum amperage.
4. Examine for silhouettes of wires, batteries, explosives, mechanisms or bomb containers.
5. If item is a closed bomb, place in bomb carrier.
6. Dismantling a closed bomb should only be done as a last resort.

Polaroid X-Ray Film Developer

1. Place film cassette adjacent to bomb on side away from x-ray tube.
2. Expose film to x-ray.

3. Carry film cassette to Polaroid film developer, away from bomb.
4. Develop film.

Listening Device

1. Place microphone near closed bomb and listen.
2. Mechanical clockwork can be heard often without amplification.
3. Corrosive delays cannot usually be heard unless chemical solution is extremely heavy. The Davis listening device allegedly can pick up a time-pencil corrosive action even when pencil is enclosed within a pipe.

Tong Opening

1. Place two pairs of tongs on bomb opposite each other.
2. Place over protrusions or in grooves.
3. Do not allow tongs to penetrate cardboard containers.
4. If bomb is smooth and hard, place tape on side and place tong teeth into tape.
5. Tie one tong to a heavy fixed object.
6. Tie other tong with a long line to rear of vehicle.
7. Drive vehicle slowly away from bomb.

Protective Shield

1. Carry shield to a safe operating distance from bomb.
2. Set up shield.
3. Attach arms and tools to arms.
4. Stay behind shield and push it to bomb.
5. Dismantle bomb.
6. Lift bomb on arm.
7. Push shield to carrier.
8. Place bomb in carrier.

Fired Projectile (Grenade Launcher)

1. For accuracy, place weapon adjacent to bomb.
2. Sandbag weapon in place.
3. Aim so that projectile will be caught harmlessly by a barrier.
4. Place projectile in or on weapon.
5. Load weapon.
6. Attach string to trigger.
7. Retreat to safe position.

8. Make sure area is evacuated.
9. Pull string to fire weapon.

Transportation

1. Uncover "Danger, Bomb" signs on vehicle.
2. Place bomb in middle of carrier.
3. Drive on least populated, smoothest roads to magazine or disposal area.

Storage

1. Store caps and triggering devices in one magazine.
2. Store bulk explosives in a separate magazine.

Blasting

1. If bomb is to be exploded in place, obtain permission from a superior officer and/or manager of location.
2. Open doors and windows; sandbag.
3. Advise evacuation.
4. Scrape oxidation off ends of blasting wire.
5. Unreel wire.
6. Use galvanometer to check open circuit for shorts.
7. Use galvanometer to check closed circuit for continuity.
8. Use galvanometer to check cap.
9. Place cap in circuit.
10. Place cap in explosive beside or on bomb.
11. Retreat to safe position at other end of blasting wire.
12. Use galvanometer to check circuit.
13. Place blasting machine in circuit.
14. Make sure area is evacuated.
15. Have assistant set up camera.
16. Turn blasting machine as hard as possible.
17. Assistant will take photograph of explosion.
18. Take a photograph of crater.
19. Search area for fragments.

Fuse Blasting

1. Cut six inches off fuse end and discard it.
2. Cut one foot of fuse for time test and burn it.
3. Cut desired length of fuse (at least three feet).

4. Remove fuse cap from box and crimp cap to fuse.
5. Remove equipment from area.
6. Place fuse lighter on fuse.
7. Make sure area is evacuated.
8. Pull fuse lighter.
9. Retreat to safe position.
10. Photograph explosion.
11. Photograph crater with ruler in it.

Chapter 8

SEARCH AND DISPOSAL OF BOMBS IN MOTOR VEHICLES

TYPES OF VEHICLE BOMBS

A variety of vehicle bombs may be encountered according to the abilities, resources, motivations, purposes and opportunities of bombers:

1. To vandalize an empty vehicle.
2. To destroy a vehicle for insurance.
3. To intimidate the owner or someone else.
4. To injure or kill the driver or passengers.
5. To kill everyone in a vehicle.
6. To kill a passerby.
7. To kill as many as possible or destroy a target in the vicinity.

More than one vehicle may have a bomb in it at one location, several locations at the same time or at delayed times. Vehicles may be automobiles, trucks, semitrailers, motorcycles, bicycles or animal powered. Cars are often used only to transport bombs to their intended targets but may also be used for concealment at targets. Vehicles may add to the fragmentation effect and a vehicle's fuel may add to the incendiary effect. (Incidentally, in normal automobile fires, rarely does the gasoline tank explode. Special effects personnel create car explosions at the request of movie directors many times and, as a result, many people think that every time there is a car fire, the car will explode. Bystanders may be afraid to assist trapped victims because they are afraid the gasoline tank may explode.)

The biggest problem in bombing protection is cars or trucks, heavily loaded with explosives, being parked adjacent to or near the intended target. The simplest form of protection against this form of attack is to use barriers of many different sorts to prevent easy access to the target. Sand-filled barrels secured with heavy connecting railings help to prevent car bombs from being parked close to targets. The barriers shown in

Figure 87 prevent traffic. The further the barriers are from the target, the more effective they are.

Figure 87. Heavy barriers block vehicle bombs from being parked adjacent to targets. Heavy rails connecting the posts are more effective. Plants and shrubbery, though, provide concealment areas for possible bombs.

Terrorists are using larger vehicle bombs, and the common practice of placing parking garages under large buildings, as shown in Figure 88, only adds to the security problem. Separate parking garages with barriers are the best answer. Barriers are more fully discussed in Chapter 11.

Upon arriving at the scene and after talking to officers or complainants, the technician may decide to wear coveralls to protect his clothing from dirt. He should carry a flashlight with him as he approaches the vehicle. The second bomb technician, at a safe distance, should take two oblique photographs of the car, showing both sides, front, rear, license tag and location of the vehicle.

Figure 88. This type of design may save money, but a bomb protection specialist would recommend separating the parking area for security.

OVERALL INSPECTION

The bomb technician should walk around the vehicle and make a general observation of the vehicle without touching it. He should examine the vehicle for possible pull wires attached from a bomb on the vehicle to a fixed object, for remote control wires, for a burning fuse as shown in Figure 89, loose wires, tape, grenade pull rings, fuse lighters, or igniters. In addition, a perpetrator may leave shoe or tire impressions, disturbed areas on the ground or fingermarks on the vehicle.

Figure 89. The mark on the asphalt where the fuse had burned may be seen to the right of the bomb. Bombers may drop matches, cigarettes, cigars, fuse lighter pull wires or lighters when using safety fuse.

Before searching further, a bomb disposal technician or bomb searcher may use an explosives detection dog or an electronic explosives vapor detector to scan the vehicle.

COMMON LOCATIONS OF BOMBS

Robots

If a small robot is available as shown in Figure 90, then the underside of a vehicle can be searched using its video camera and light. Some other robots have long extension arms that may reach under vehicles. The wheelbarrow robot was the first to be able to place a tow bar and heavy line under a vehicle and detach the tow bar in order to allow a tow truck to move a vehicle suspected of containing a bomb. In vehicles that are suspected of containing bombs, robots are also used to penetrate the vehicle's windows. Robots can also fire a bullet into a vehicle's trunk in order to place a piece of detonating cord and detonator there. The small resulting explosion opens the vehicle for further inspection but is hard on the vehicle and may detonate any explosives located in the vehicle.

Figure 90. This little robot takes a lot of the work and hazard out of searching under vehicles for bombs. With an extension arm, it can search between the seats of aircraft and overhead luggage compartments. An electronic sniffer attachment on it can detect explosive vapors as well as do visual searching.

A bomb disposal technician or a bomb searcher may routinely use a mirror and light on an extension pole to routinely search under vehicles that are admitted to a limited access area.

The laser fiber optic flexible light with a mirror and magnifier is helpful in examining dark, hard-to-see or hard-to-reach areas of automobiles as well as in suspect package bombs.

The most common place for a bomb in a motor vehicle is under the hood on the left side of the engine. This bomb uses an electric cap for a primer, which is initiated by the ignition system (Figs. 91 and 92). The best method for locating this type of bomb is to lie on one's back and slide under the left side of the vehicle as far as possible and, using a flashlight, look up into the motor compartment for a bomb, explosive, wire, fuse, or anything unusual about the vehicle (Figures 93, 94 and 95). Then the technician will get up and finish the observation of the underside of the vehicle by sliding under its front, right and rear sides. He should check the top of the muffler, exhaust pipe, gas tank, inside the bumpers and frame or anyplace under the car where explosives may be concealed. Figures 96 and 97 show two typical car bombings intended to kill or injure the driver.

Figure 91. This was one of the first bombs that the author dismantled. The several sticks of dynamite can be seen on the left side of the engine against the fire wall. Removal by a robot, or severing wires with a robot, or dismantling with a disrupter would be the safest method today.

Bombs have been located in, or adjacent to, automobile gas tanks. Corrosive-delay-initiated bombs may be dropped into gas tanks. One extortion attempt in Dade County was made by securing a plastic soap dish with thermite and plastic explosive under a gas tank with magnets. Edges of the gas tank bent inward indicated the force was directed from the outside. This method is taught in sabotage schools and the consequences are shown in Figure 98.

ENTERING

The hood of the automobile may be raised by remote control, using ropes, levers and fulcrums. In his monograph, Newhouser goes into

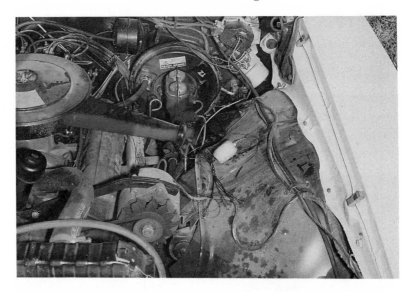

Figure 92. This bomb consisted of a lump of C4 and an electric cap that was found by the owner of this vehicle and which was located on the left side of his engine. The bomb was dismantled by Police Technician Gerald Reichardt, before robots and disrupters come into use.

detail on this method and on the complete search of every part of the vehicle. If there are large numbers of calls of this nature, then the technician may save time but take a risk by lifting the hood manually. If he does, it should be done slowly and he should watch closely as he unlatches and raises the hood. Pressure-release and pull-device bombs can be easily adapted to explode when a hood is raised. Automobile burglar alarms activated when automobiles are moved or when a door, hood or trunk is opened may be the initiator for a bomb.

My former partner, Bomb Specialist and Criminalist Newton Porter, who was one of the first graduates of the Hazardous Devices School, devised many improvements on the remote opening of vehicles. He was motivated to do so because the first bomb he dismantled was a radio-controlled bomb attached to the gasoline tank of an automobile. He not only dismantled the bomb, but he was able to develop the fingerprints of the suspect from inside the bomb. The car belonged to a witness in a drug case. For his efforts, Newton Porter and his assistant, Jerry Lauck, both were awarded the first of two citations for Officer of the Year.

Now that robots have been developed, any action that can be performed remotely with a robot should be done so. Any one or more of the following actions can and should be done with a robot, if feasible:

Figure 93. The effects of a powerful car bomb can be seen in this photo. The bomb was concealed in the engine compartment and the driver had no indication that it was there until the bomb exploded, causing the loss of the driver's legs. This type of bomb is designed to kill or injure the vehicle's driver.

Figure 94. This bomb exploded on top of the car hood with no one in the car. If possible, a bomb scene should be vacuumed and the sweepings carefully examined in the laboratory.

Figure 95. One of the most commonly overlooked clues at bombings is fingerprints. In this bombing, the perpetrator(s) may have leaned against the car while placing the bomb on the hood.

Figure 96. When the victim turned on the ignition key, "everything started twisting and turning," which is a good description of an explosion by the victim, who lived. This powerful explosion blew down the doors on the courtyard wall as well as the front of the house. The hood of the car landed in the back yard.

Figure 97. This is the vehicle shown in Figure 96. The entire left side of the engine disintegrated. A four-inch fragment of a cap wire was found under the rear bumper.

searching a vehicle for a suspect bomb, opening a vehicle suspected of containing a bomb, photographing a vehicle or a suspect bomb, looking for evidence, removing a suspect bomb from a vehicle and dismantling a suspect item.

Bombs that have failed to explode but have been submitted to an electrical impulse from the ignition system of the vehicle may explode while or after being disconnected.

In some instances, the complainant has found a bomb or an item he thinks is a bomb in his own vehicle. It is not necessary to search for the bomb but just to dispose of it. Of course, this should be done remotely and with a disrupter, if possible. Disrupters cause damage to vehicles occasionally, so some type of financial responsibility might be arranged with the owner before disrupting. Often just advising the owner, "This procedure may damage the car, but there is no other method of safely removing the bomb. If you wish to remove the bomb yourself, you may do so, but it may cause fatal injuries," is sufficient for the owner to pay for the damage.

Some of the best ways of preventing the placement of bombs in

Figure 98. Shown is an extortion bombing. The bomb had been placed under the gas tank to explode while the complainant was asleep. The edges of the metal surrounding the hole were bent inwards, indicating the bomb was on the outside of the gas tank. The author has disposed of over one hundred of these types of bombs, mostly recovered from terrorist organizations.

vehicles are burglar alarms, electrical cutoff switches, or remote starters as commonly used in cold climates. Most vehicles now have the hood release inside the driving compartment which helps prevent easy access to the engine compartment.

The least commonly used door on an automobile is the right rear, especially if the car is a two-door (a little humor). The technician should first observe the inside of the right rear door through the windows on the opposite side of the vehicle. If he does not notice anything unusual, he should next enter the automobile by this door. All other doors are then opened from the inside. Entry into the trunk may be effected by removing the rear seat if raising of the trunk lid is suspected of being the initiating action of a bomb.

The most effective place to hide a bomb is under the driver's seat, which also is the second most common area where bombs have been placed, as determined from a study of past cases. In July, 1970, Sergeant Cote of Montreal dismantled a bomb protruding from beneath the right front seat of a vehicle. Concealed on the rear floor and in the front trunk of the vehicle was more dynamite, to compose a total explosive bomb weight of 150 pounds.

The bomb in the Ford Econoline which exploded at the University of Wisconsin in August, 1970, consisted of several hundred pounds of ammonium nitrate and fuel in the rear of the vehicle.

Since that time, vehicle bombs have increased in size and frequency in attempts to kill and destroy targets throughout the world. Bombs weighing several hundred pounds are common. The largest vehicle bomb was dismantled in the United Kingdom. The truck contained tons of explosives. Suicide drivers and proxy drivers are additional problems with which to contend. Proxy drivers are innocents, who are forced to deliver a bomb to a location before a hostage is killed. Mortars and rockets on vehicles have been concealed at distances from targets. These mortars or rockets are delivered by bombers utilizing timers or radio control. Restricted parking and vigorous searching patrols, with vapor detectors, are used to help protect such suspected targets as airports and government centers. Figure 99 shows a controlled parking zone in Belfast.

Examination of the area under the seats may be preceded by examination of the floor mats for lumps and displacement. Seats should be examined for lumps and openings in the upholstery. One lucky victim found a bomb in his vehicle because of an uncomfortable lump in his car seat, which was caused by a bomb wedged into it. The incident occurred in New York.

The area under the dashboard should be examined next and the glove compartment opened. For final examination, the vehicle is started, moved in all gears and all accessories are turned on. A detailed search of the interiors of air conditioners and hubcaps might reveal a bomb, but no cases of bombs in these locations have been authenticated. Figure 100 depicts a car bombing with a message.

REMOVAL

Unless the bomb specialist is sure of the method of initiating a bomb found in a car, he may first move it or break connecting wires by remote control with a line and a fish hook. A device with a battery-powered relay may be activated by removing any wires. Newhouser depicts a method of breaking the battery connection by placing a jumper cable on one battery post, removing the battery cable and pulling the jumper cable loose with a line from a distance.

Figure 99. Unattended vehicles parked in control zones can be opened by the application of a small amount of explosive.

MOTOR VEHICLE SEARCH CHECKLIST

The following steps are a guide and will vary with the individual situation. If possible, use a robot for preliminary examination and opening of a vehicle.

Upon Arrival

1. Talk to the first officer at the scene, complainant, or officer in charge.
2. Find out why anyone thinks there is a bomb in the vehicle.
3. Make sure the area is kept evacuated.

Figure 100. The bomber confessed to the author that he had performed a dozen bombings and had been coerced into many of them. The bomber became a reliable informant and lectured to a class on bombing investigation before he was murdered.

Assistant

1. Provides necessary tools and equipment.
2. Takes two photographs of vehicle from a distance, showing both sides, rear, front, tag, vehicle identification number and any distinguishing tags if it can be done without risk.
3. Take photographs of spectators.

General Observation

1. Walk around vehicle without touching it.
2. Look for pull wires, loose wiring, tape, unknown objects, shoe impressions, visible finger marks and look through windows.
3. Look for pressure or pressure-release devices under wheels.
4. Examine fuel-filler tube for explosives, wire, tape or foreign matter.

Underneath

1. Use a mirror and flashlight to look under vehicle before getting underneath.
2. Technician lies on his or her back and slides under the driver's side of the engine.
3. Use flashlight and mirror to look up into the motor compartment and under the driver's seat.
4. Slide back out and slide under the front, other side and rear of vehicle.
5. Search top of muffler, exhaust pipe, end of exhaust pipe, bumpers, fuel tank and chassis for explosives, wire, fuse, tape or anything unusual.

Engine

1. Open hood slowly and remotely, if possible.
2. The hood release is now commonly found inside a vehicle and can be opened remotely.
3. The technician may wish to disconnect the battery by attaching another cable to it with a clamp, cutting or unbolting the regular battery terminal and pulling off his own clamp, remotely.
4. Examine engine compartment thoroughly.

Interior

1. Look through the opposite windows for extraneous materials attached to opposite doors.
2. Windows may be remotely broken, or keys used, with a robot to open doors. This takes practice.
3. Car door remote-opening tools may be prefabricated for almost any vehicle.
4. Examine with a light and mirror under the driver's seat and other seats.
5. Look for openings in seats, bulges and loose wires, tape or unknown objects.
6. Examine floors, dash and all compartments.

Trunk

1. May be released from inside of vehicle, but try to do this remotely.
2. Entry to the trunk may be obtained by removing the rear seat.

3. Entry to the trunk may be done with a key in the hand of some robots or with a remote key or door openers.

Moving Parts

1. Start vehicle motor.
2. Move vehicle in all gears.
3. Let motor idle.
4. Turn on all switches, handles and push all buttons.

Results

No Bomb Found

1. Advise police and complainant if *no bomb was found.*
2. Do *not advise* that there is no bomb in vehicle.

Bomb Located

1. Photograph bomb in place.
2. Do not cut wires.
3. Break wires and remove remotely with rope.
4. Do not cut wires or remove battery cable if bomb fires by collapsing circuit.
5. Pull bomb out of car with ropes, by remote control if possible.

Chapter 9

COMMERCIAL EXPLOSIVES AND
MILITARY ORDNANCE

PRECAUTIONS

The bomb technician, when responding to any call which requires the collection of explosives or suspected explosives, should take his bomb truck to the scene. You must remember that the complainant or police officer at the scene is often unfamiliar with explosives and will hazard erroneous guesses, often stating that he has found explosives when actually the item is a dangerous bomb. Secondly, the explosive may be in such a sensitive condition that it may explode while being moved as shown in Figures 101 and 102.

Movement

Persons finding suspected bombs will often move them outside or will bring these items to the police station themselves rather than wait for the bomb squad to arrive at the scene. This conduct should be met with strong warnings and renewed training to police officers concerning the risks in moving explosives.

The bomb technician should carefully examine the item before touching it, since the explosive may be a bomb, or booby trap or decoy for the real bomb, and the person at the scene may not realize it. Movement of items around it may explode the bomb accidentally. If the item is a suspected bomb, bomb procedures should be used.

An item believed to be so sensitive to initiation that it may explode upon being moved should be photographed first so that it can still be identified later, even if it does explode.

Figure 101. The ruler indicates 1½ inches of nitroglycerine that has exuded into the bottom of this case of dynamite. It is thick, oily and yellowish. There were eight similar boxes of dynamite about ten years old. The quantity of the material helped to absorb any shock. The most sensitive condition of NG occurs when a thin layer is applied between two pieces of steel.

Figure 102. When an individual injures himself experimenting with improvised explosives, always search his bedroom, workshop or vehicle for other dangerous and sensitive ingredients like these.

Identifying an Explosive

When it is difficult to determine whether the item is an explosive, a simple test may be conducted by taking a pea-size sample and placing it on a piece of paper. The remainder should be placed at a safe distance. The paper should be lit and the flame observed as it approaches the suspected material. The specialist stands back approximately three feet. If the material flares up, torches or sparkles, the remainder should be treated as an explosive. This test can usually be performed safely in an ashtray in an office, since rarely will you encounter an explosive that when unconfined will explode when such a small specimen is burned. Some explosives are difficult to ignite, and if the sample does not burn, however, one cannot conclude that the specimen is not explosive. Of course, you should not attempt to test any sample in a fragile container. Heat should never be applied to blasting caps or suspected red phosphorus and potassium chlorate mixtures. Figure 103 shows a spot test for suspected explosives.

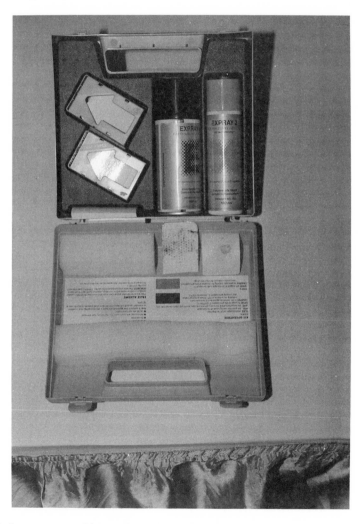

Figure 103. A compact test kit may be easily carried and stored in a bomb squad vehicle for examination of suspected explosives.

Hypergolic Mixtures

A few words should be inserted here concerning red phosphorus and potassium chlorate. They compose what is known as a hypergolic mixture, which means that the two substances may explode upon being mixed together. This may not happen at once, but they may explode after a while all by themselves. The slightest movement may initiate a "violent reaction," as the chemical companies state on the containers. (Figure 105 "Violent reaction" is an understatement, as exemplified by the following incidents.)

A bottle of this mixture was left on a detective's desk in New York City by another detective who did not know what it was. While the room was unoccupied, the mixture exploded spontaneously, breaking windows, light fixtures and the desk top.

A boy in Dade County had the majority of the friction skin on his hands, fingers and stomach scarred while placing approximately one ounce of the material into a plastic capsule.

The writer received second- and third-degree burns on 25 percent of his body and had an eardrum blown out while disposing of one pound of the same material which was left from the previous incident. Since the chemicals were unconfined on newspaper which he held, the effects were not more critical. Figure 104 shows the containers after the incident.

Three officers in Canada were injured while attempting to burn small quantities of this mixture on a shovel blade.

A Cuban revolutionary bomber in Miami lost 50 percent of his hearing in one ear and 100 percent in the other ear when the front of his body from the waist up was blackened from the explosion of a red phosphorus mixture in a six-ounce can, which was being made into a homemade incendiary grenade. The scene is depicted in Figure 105.

A chemistry teacher lost a finger when less than an ounce of his red phosphorus, potassium nitrate and thermite mixture exploded in a beaker while he was carrying it from one room to another.

A writer of a book telling how to make bombs lost all his fingers on one hand with an ounce of this same mixture. When the mixture is made with alcohol, it is known as Armstrong's reagent and may explode after the alcohol evaporates or when it is disturbed. In the eighties, drug dealers in some parts of the country began experimenting with phosphorous and chlorate mixtures. It is imperative that these mixtures be treated with the utmost caution. Do not pick them up with bare hands or

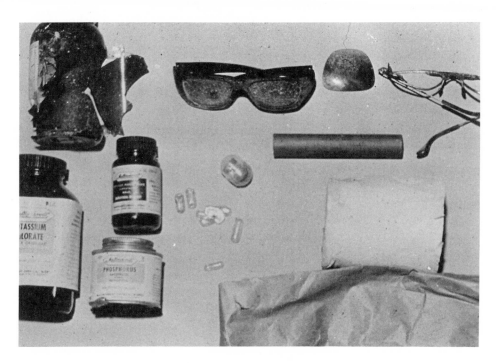

Figure 104. This photograph was taken of the empty containers of material that exploded and injured the author.

hold them in front of your face for examination. They may explode spontaneously or with the slightest agitation or heat. Distance and barriers are the best forms of protection.

When possible, it is best to use a robot to examine, desensitize or move suspected red phosphorous and potassium chlorate mixtures. The mixture should be wet with an equivalent volume or more of water before removing it. Never allow the two chemicals to mix if they are found in separate containers.

Disposal of this mixture is best performed while wearing a bomb suit and it is necessary to wet the mixture with an equivalent volume of water before removing it. Disposal of the separate ingredients is simply performed by dumping the red phosphorus on paper and the potassium chlorate in a cardboard box with a good bottom in it, placing the box over the phosphorus. A long fuse inserted into the phosphorus will ignite it, and it will burn slowly through the box and into the potassium chlorate.

White phosphorus and yellow phosphorus are usually stored underwater. When they dry out, they will burn almost immediately in some

Figure 105. The author soaked this red phosphorous mixture with water before removing it, and even then smoke emanated from it.

instances or some time later if the phosphorus is old and has a coating on it.

Sodium is similar to phosphorus in appearance when broken into small chunks. Sodium, however, is stored under kerosene or oil, or in airtight aluminum containers. Upon contact with water, it will explode. If large quantities are to be destroyed, large bodies of water are needed, since the sodium scatters in pieces for repeated explosions. On the ground, sodium may merely bubble to form a coating until the next time it rains, which may cause it to explode if the coating is then broken.

Bomb squads are often called upon to dispose of old chemicals and dangerous materials. A good reference book, *Dangerous Properties of Industrial Materials,* edited by I. N. Sax (3rd ed, New York, Reinhold), carried in the bomb truck when it is used, may prevent serious injury to the bomb technician.

IDENTIFICATION OF TYPE

Requests for disposal of explosives are common in areas where large quantities are used in quarrying (South Florida), mining (Colorado) or road construction through mountains. When discarded, stolen or illegal explosives or explosives from bombs are found, the information obtained from a complete description of what is found may help solve a theft or apprehend bombers (Fig. 106). The type of explosive, size, color, approximate weight, labels, batch number, manufacturer and exact count should be listed in one's report (Fig. 107). If the technician believes the material is too sensitive for too much handling, he may decide to dispense with this procedure.

Figure 106. A cloth bag filled with 60 pounds of dynamite was left in a Goodwill Industries box adjacent to a grocery store. It was retrieved after someone made an anonymous telephone call. The manufacturer of this dynamite was identified and it was determined that it had been stolen two years previously. Several bombers have turned explosives over to authorities willingly, with the understanding that no questions would be asked.

In order to identify a material that is suspected of being explosive or to determine its source, it may be helpful and advisable to contact the Bureau of Alcohol, Tobacco and Firearms. The BATF is under the Treasury Department and works in conjunction with the Federal Bureau of Investigation's National Bomb Data Center to assist other agencies in the identification of explosives. A computerized program can be contacted by dialing a toll-free telephone number, which is (800) 800-3855, twenty-four hours a day. A complete description may not only identify the material but also may provide precautions and assistance in an investigation and disposal. The United Kingdom has the best collection of small samples of live explosives.

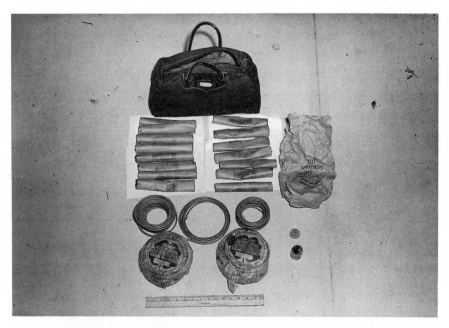

Figure 107. This cache of dynamite and caps was found under a store. The blasting caps, fuse and dynamite were the same type used by a right-wing bombing group in an attempted bombing of a synagogue. This information was used in the trial of a ringleader.

Caps

Information obtained from blasting caps should include length, color and diameter of the cap, the type of crimp at the top of the cap (if it is an electric cap) and whether it has a round or dimpled bottom (Fig. 108). The type and color of the plug, as well as the length of the wires and color of the insulation, also assist in identifying the manufacturer. The sι, int or clip which holds the opposite ends of the leg wires are distinctly different with each manufacturer. Some large manufacturers may produce a line of caps for another company with that company's name on them. Delay caps have one label or tag on the wires indicating the amount of time of the delay and in some instances will also have the length of the wires stamped on the tag. Since approximately 1963, all manufacturers mark caps on the side as "blasting cap dangerous explosive." The color of the writing is different with each company. In addition, each company will have different colors of wires and labels on different types of caps. Fuse caps are usually not crimped to fuse by the maker in the United States. The incident in Figure 109 is a rare event. Also, the color of the flash powder inside the fuse caps will help in their identification. Never insert a probe into a fuse cap to examine the powder more closely. This material is as sensitive as a match is to friction, and caps will almost always remove fingers in contact explosions. Some cap factories use paper or cardboard sleeves to hold the wires in their accordion fold.

Figure 108. This collection of known standard live caps and fuse was submitted to the Bureau of Alcohol, Tobacco and Firearms to help start their live reference collection of standards.

Formerly, only boxes of explosives had lot numbers on them, and the individual cartridges or sticks of explosives did not. Now, the cartridges have a date plant shift code on them, and accurate records that should be maintained by manufacturers, distributors and users. The problem is insufficient inspection of magazines and job sites. The solution lies in more personnel and assistance by local bomb squads in inspections. The Bureau of Alcohol, Tobacco and Firearms has provided a much needed service in enforcing federal regulations.

Every case of dynamite and every box of blasting caps has an instruction sheet in it. This sheet contains the same information which is on the individual items and states the safety rules in the use of explosives as well as how to use the dynamite or cap. This is a standard form drawn up by the Institute of the Makers of Explosives, but every company has its own printer and has its name printed on the bottom of the front page of

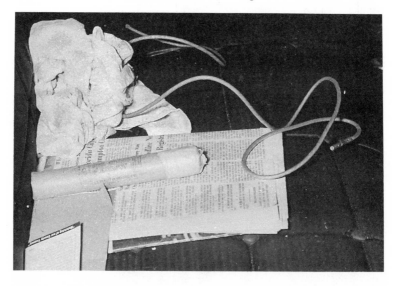

Figure 109. This bomb was found on the front seat of a political candidate's automobile. When the cap was extracted from the dynamite by the author, teeth marks were found on it. Instead of crimping the cap at the top, the bomber chewed the length of the cap like corn on the cob. He was fortunate the cap did not explode in his mouth.

this sheet. A series of railroad bombings were solved in Florida through two items found at the scene of a train bombing: a shunt from an electric blasting cap and the instruction sheet from a case of dynamite. Information had been received on who had stolen the explosives from the same manufacturer. The perpetrators blew up several trestles and trains, as shown in Figures 110 and 111, before they were apprehended.

Fuse

The Ensign Bickford Company formerly manufactured most of the fuse used in this country. Now, almost all of the safety fuse used in the United States is of foreign manufacture. Fuse is seldom used in commercial blasting and consequently it is less often used in bombings. At one time, fuse and fuse caps were the primary means of bomb initiation. Authorities requesting disposal, frequently, mistakenly identified safety fuse with detonating cord. The best determination is examination of the core at the end. If the core is white, it is detonating cord; if the core is black, it is safety fuse. Safety fuse has a black powder core and will burn at approximately 120 sec/yd or 90 sec/yd ± 10 percent. The exterior normally is found in three different colors, for contrast with the back-

Figure 110. Approximately fifty pounds of dynamite exploded under the train trestle about eight feet in front of this locomotive which was traveling about sixty miles an hour. The windshield and lights broke and rails were caught in the cowcatcher.

ground. These are orange, white or black fiber. The military fuse, M700, has a dark green, plastic cover for camouflage, increased waterproofing and prevention of damage. This fuse is designed to burn underwater and can even be ignited underwater with a military fuse lighter. Safety fuse is also called time fuse or dynamite fuse. The manufacturer states that less than two feet of fuse should not be used and also gives other safety rules. Violations of these rules have resulted in deaths of three blasters in Dade County in two separate cases. Bombs recovered from Cuban revolutionaries in the Miami area have been found with four-inch fuses (Fig. 112). Reloaded grenades with a two-inch fuse for a time delay were recovered in one bomb factory which produced the items for sale to Castro in 1958 (Figs. 113). Short fuses are often used when a person is illegally fishing with dynamite, and such a mistake results in the loss of hands. Fuse is manufactured in fifty-foot lengths, so the maximum burning time possible without splicing two lengths together is approximately 33 minutes.

Figure 111. The locomotive traveled 100 feet before stopping. Thirty-three railroad cars piled up in the crater and caught fire. Sergeant Al Coutts found the initiating switch in the bottom of the crater at Point 2. At Point 1 a shunt and an instruction sheet were found.

Figure 112. These aerial bombs were seized by customs agents from a Cuban exile organization as they were loading them onto an airplane in a tomato field. There were 33⅓ pounds of dynamite and it was wrapped with tape and covered with blankets. The caps had four-inch (ten second) fuses on them.

One bomber in Miami left 25 feet of fuse stretched out across the lawn. Figure 114 shows the bombing of the Soviet Embassy in Washington, D.C.

The manufacturer of fuse can be determined by a count of the fiber wrappings. The Federal Bureau of Investigation Laboratory has an extensive collection of fuse and blasting caps to assist in the identification of unknown products. Figure 115 shows a roll of safety fuse.

Non-Electric Detonators

Non-electric detonators is a term that the armed forces used for fuse caps, or detonators, that are crimped to safety fuse initiated by flame or fuse lighters. Now the commercial makers have adopted the term to mean a non-electric initiation system of shock tubing with a detonator attached to it by the manufacturer. This thin clear plastic tubing as shown in Figure 66 is usually initiated by the blaster with a hand-held firing device. The tubing is not destructive because it contains only a small amount of fine reactive material in powdered or gas form. This tubing may be called signal tubing and can be attached to detonating cord or blasting caps which will initiate it. The detonator that is attached to the end of the shock tube will initiate

Figure 113. Three Americans had a lively business of reloading old grenades with shotgun primers, safety fuse and black powder. The grenades were being sold to Castro while Batista was still in power.

boosters, detonating cord or cap-sensitive bulk explosives. Shock tubing can be attached to other pieces of shock tubing.

This form of initiation of explosives utilizing a shot-shell hand-held firing device is not conducive to the purpose of many types of bombings. The perpetrator usually has to be at the scene at the time of the bombing.

Detonating Cord

Prima cord is an Ensign Bickford brand name for detonating cord (called det cord, for short). Now the detonating cord used in the United States may be manufactured here or abroad. The purpose of det cord is to connect explosive charges together. The material explodes at 21,000 ft/sec and will insure detonation of cartridges of dynamite in holes in the ground, even if dirt gets in between the cartridges. The insulation comes in many different colors in both fiber or plastic. Formerly, detonating cord was the only method of insuring simultaneous detonation of charges without using electric caps in a circuit. It is found in 500-, 1,000- and 2,000-foot rolls. It can be easily tied together for propagation of the explosive wave.

Three bombers in Dade County have utilized detonating cord for more than one target. An alleged jewel thief had a car and boat blown up in his front yard by two connected charges (Figs. 116, 117, and 118). A

Figure 114. This bomb was placed on the inside windowsill of the Soviet Embassy by a Cuban exile from Miami. The fuse was so short that the blast knocked the bomber down as he was leaving the scene.

Cuban boat manufacturer had two boats destroyed by three spaced charges (Figs. 119 and 120). Figure 121 shows a ship that had two holes blown in it. Boats confiscated by customs were blown up by Cubans who stretched the cord from the boats to the street so that they could make a quick getaway after lighting the fuse (Figs. 122, 123 and 124). Four legs of a microwave tower in Nevada were blown up by connecting detonating cord. School buses in Colorado were also blown up in a similar method.

Dynamite

The manufacture and use of dynamite in commercial blasting has become rare in the United States. It is being replaced by emulsions. Only about three percent of the four billion pounds of explosives used yearly in the United States is cap-sensitive. This makes the explosives industry safer and less costly, but also makes it more difficult for bombers to steal or buy explosives.

Figure 115. The most common bomb in the United States used to be sections of fuse cut from a roll of safety fuse as shown on the edge of the table. Fuse caps were attached to the fuse by the bombers and inserted into explosives of different kinds, including one-pound primers as shown. Now the most common bomb is a pipe bomb, thanks to better controls and improvements in explosives.

For recognition purposes, dynamite is found in round, straight cylinders of paper or cardboard or semi-rigid plastic. The paper or cardboard cylinders are folded or crimped over on each end and are coated with wax. The colors vary from brown to white or red. The writing on the cartridges vary in color from black to red and blue, through the years. Some dynamites are used in oil exploration and for primers for non-cap-sensitive explosives. This has helped vary the length of dynamite cartridges from four inches to over five feet.

The color of the contents of a stick is from light brown to dark brown. Flecks of white or yellow may be seen.

The hardness of dynamite is in accordance with its components; it may be hard or mushy. The contents of the cartridge may be dry and powdery or like a plastic, sticky mass.

Feeling the contents of a cartridge will leave the fingers oily, as nitroglycerine is an oil. Also dynamite has a characteristic sweet odor, and some dynamites smell stronger than others. In addition, dynamite

Figure 116. Arrows 1 and 2 indicate craters of two explosive charges that exploded simultaneously, damaging a boat and a car. Notice boat in the backyard and surrounding area.

Figure 117. Arrow indicates fragment of a time pencil that stuck in the rafter above the explosion. A cleared path across the ground was made by det cord.

will give the person who handles it a headache. One Cuban bomb group, obviously with limited knowledge of explosives, upon examination of fake dynamite given to them by an informant said, "This is good dynamite. It doesn't even give you a headache." Dynamite is salty to the taste.

Frequently in climates such as South Florida, where there is high heat and humidity, the oxidizing salts (sodium nitrate and ammonium nitrate) pick up moisture from the air and the dynamite is therefore ruined

Figure 118. Two days after the bomb in the front yard, someone placed a bomb in a well-known boat docked in the rear of the house. Arrow indicates the author searching for evidence in the canal.

Figure 119. Ten thousand dollars damage was caused by this bomb which consisted of three explosive charges connected with det cord. This was the last of three bombings at the same location. Bombers sometimes return to the scene to see the effects or to bomb again.

rapidly (Fig. 125). This moisture will desensitize it. A case in Coral Gables involving the bombing of a judge's home had a happy ending because of this. The dynamite had been stolen eight weeks previous to

Figure 120. On a previous bombing attempt a bomb consisting of 1½ pounds of C4 in a toilet tissue bag and an inverted time pencil was found on the front doorstep. The cap exploded harmlessly. This is an extortion type of bomb or an attention-getting device.

Figure 121. This ship in the Miami River had two holes blown in the hull below the waterline on the starboard side. In the vacant lot to the right side of the photograph and beyond the fence line of the facility, a paper bag containing a diver's hood and glove were found.

the attempted explosion. The perpetrator(s) cut the 2 inches × 2 ft sticks to sixteen inches to fit inside a beer box. However, the open twenty pounds of dynamite became very moist because the victim suffered a

Figure 122. Two burned pieces of fuse and fuse lighters can be seen in the foreground. Detonating cord from caps leading to the main charge broke the concrete block. A four-inch piece of cord broke off along a 100-foot path, at the place where two pieces of cord had been tied together.

Figure 123. The det cord path led directly to the boats that were destroyed by this large blast.

heart attack and was in the hospital, forcing the bomber to postpone his action for eight weeks. The night he came home from the hospital, the

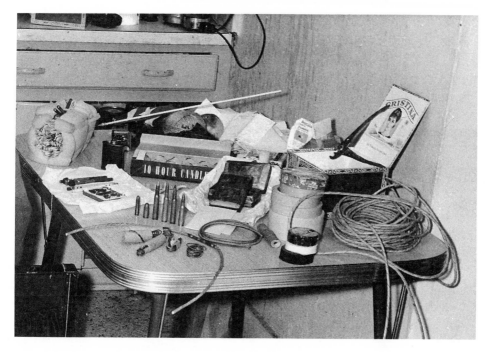

Figure 124. A search of an injured suspect's house disclosed the bomb-maker's kit shown here which included explosive and thermite-filled soap dishes.

victim heard the bang of two blasting caps and an alarm clock ringing. The moist dynamite was splattered all over the front of the house (Figs. 126, 127, and 128). Someone released information to the news media stating why the bomb failed to explode, but luckily, the bomber never attempted to rectify his mistake from this information. Years later, the exterior of the judge's house was brightly illuminated.

The moisture that exudes from the dynamite is not pure nitroglycerine. It is a mixture of water and salts with the oily nitroglycerine seen floating on the surface (Fig. 129). If the liquid is allowed to sit in proper condition and if the dynamite has a high percentage of nitroglycerine (NG), the water may evaporate, leaving only NG. (Nitroglycerine is not called "nitro," because this may also refer to nitro carbo nitrate.)

Old dynamite, in various stages of decomposition, will be found in the future for many years and will have to be handled by bomb squads.

Figure 125. Two bombers for a labor union were sentenced for possession of this dynamite which they left in their apartment. Fingerprints of one suspect were found on the newspaper.

Blasting Agents

Nitro carbo nitrate, or NCN, is now more often called ANFO because fuel oil has become the most common fuel that is added to ammonium nitrate to make it a blasting agent. Ammonium nitrate by itself is an oxidizer. ANFO is found that is marked oxidizer or may be found unmarked. ANFO is not found in cartridges smaller than two inches in diameter and it looks similar to large cartridges of dynamite. It is packed in polyethylene bags within cardboard tubes, as shown in Figure 130. ANFO comes in either white or pink prills (granules). It needs confinement for best results upon explosion and usually requires a booster with a blasting cap or detonator. Figure 131 is a booster used by itself. Figure 132 was a bomb which only the booster exploded. However, some ANFO may be found that will explode unconfined or with just a blasting cap even though it is not supposed to do so.

Ninety-seven percent of the explosives made and used in the United States are not cap-sensitive. They are called blasting agents which are

Figure 126. In this photo, the two blasting caps exploded, scattering 20 pounds of moist dynamite over the front of the house, where only six feet away children were sleeping. Bombers are truly vicious criminals.

chemical mixtures of oxidizers and fuels. The two components are often mixed in tank-type trucks that pump the explosives into the ground at blasting sites.

Emulsion Explosives

Emulsion explosives are the same as emulsion blasting agents, except they can be exploded with a blasting cap or detonator. That includes the detonator that is found on shock tubes. It can also be exploded with certain strengths of detonating cord. An emulsion explosive is made by dissolving oxidizers (i.e. ammonium nitrate or sodium nitrate) in water and surrounding it with air bubbles, glass, oil, gum arabic, aluminum, or other fuels and oxidizers and water-resistant materials. Emulsions are sometimes referred to as water gels or slurries.

Emulsion explosives are placed in plastic tubes and crimped on the ends with ties so that the explosive cartridge looks like sausages. The plastic may be placed into cardboard tubes for reinforcing. The individual cartridges are marked with a date, plant and shift code. The plastic

Figure 127. Exact reproduction of this package bomb shows a very nondescript exterior.

container may be clear, white or colored. The explosive may be soft or hard and may appear to be a fine powder, granular, or similar to an oily pudding. The color of the explosive ranges from white to different shades of brown to gray or black.

Leaking containers of emulsion explosives or emulsion blasting agents are not sensitive like leaking cartridges of dynamite and do not have to be treated with extreme care. They are explosive and should be handled accordingly. Emulsions do not cause headaches to handlers as dynamite does.

Boosters

Boosters or primers are generally in the form of cylinders ranging in size from two ounces up to five pounds (Fig. 133). The primer may be 75 percent dynamite, also. All known boosters have a hole through the center for insertion of a blasting cap or detonation cord (Fig. 134). Primers are cast in pliable or brittle form and may be found in various shades of red or brown. These boosters may be without containers or may be supplied in cardboard wrappers, plastic or even metal cans for seismograph or water work. Primers may have date, plant, or shift code

Figure 128. The position of wires discloses that some of the wires were just used to hold the dynamite in place. Cutting wires on the outside of the package may have caused movement of the clock and the circuit wires, making a contact and detonation. Notice that the clock and battery were painted black after assembly of the bomb. This signature was duplicated in civil rights bombings sixteen years later.

nomenclature on them. Boosters are made of TNT, PETN or RDX binary explosives, forming a pentolite or a composition B explosive.

Nitroglycerine

Nitroglycerine has been found in only two cases in Dade County and may be employed in areas of the country where there are oil wells. The only time it might be encountered is when a misguided individual has made it himself or extracted it from dynamite. Since it is not the province of this book to tell how to make explosives or bombs, I will elaborate on the disposal of the material instead.

Figure 135 shows a safe burglary with explosives.

Nitroglycerine has several identifying characteristics. It is an oil, and if the fingers touch it and are rubbed together, they will be slippery. NG is very sweet to the taste; however, tasting any unknown substance is hazardous, since it may be poisonous. One should barely touch NG with his finger and then put his tongue to the end of the finger so that only a

Figure 129. This case of dynamite was so moist that when gasoline was ignited over it, the dynamite would not burn. Another case of the same dynamite was exploded when a good stick of dynamite was used as a primer and the dynamite was confined underground.

small amount is obtained. The color of newly made NG is clear or slightly yellow. When it ages, it has brown streaks in it, and when it is very old, it will have maroon streaks. The following example is illustrated in Figure 136. Two ounces of NG found in the motel room of a safe burglar in North Miami Beach was completely maroon in color. When the man was shot to death in Louisville, Kentucky, he had a bottle of NG with maroon streaks in his pocket. The two-ounce bottle that he had had in South Florida was shaken by a police officer to determine if it was NG. Later, when detonated with a blasting cap, the material left a four-foot crater.

Nitroglycerine will float in drops on water, but it will not mix with water. In fact, to move it in dynamite factories, it is pumped with water. Nitroglycerine also gives a headache to anyone who handles it unless the person has built up immunity by handling it regularly. Some people are affected by this headache more than others. A long exposure to NG will cause weakness, nausea and, one day later, may cause sore knees. The headache is caused by dilation of the blood vessels which causes a decrease in blood pressure. It is best cured by taking a shower and drinking coffee or taking No-Doz® pills which contain caffeine.

Figure 130. The late Lieutenant Fred Mowry, a pioneer in the mixing of explosives on job sites, displaying a large cartridge of NCN.

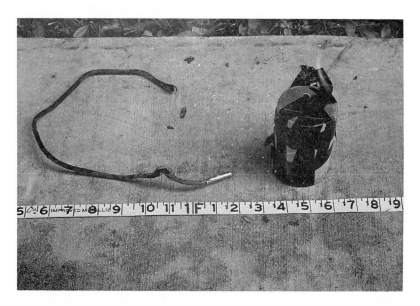

Figure 131. The author dismantled this booster bomb that had misfired in an extortion case. The house was staked out, and two days later the subjects were apprehended when they fired shots at the house. Bombers may return to view damage or if they do not accomplish their purpose.

Figure 132. The bomber left the car battery and wires at the scene. The rope had been used to lift the bomb to the roof of the target. Two large cartridges of NCN failed to explode because they lacked confinement.

To test whether or not a substance is NG, a drop of it may be burned on a piece of paper. If it does not burn, chances are that it may just be water or another chemical. Testing by striking a drop of it on metal with a hammer may result in a broken hammer and the tester being knocked over backwards, as happened to one laboratory technician.

Disposal is accomplished with a solution of nitroglycerine desensitizer or sawdust. Two solutions, A (1½ qt of water and 1 lb of sodium sulphide) and B (3½ qt of denatured alcohol and 1 qt of acetone), are kept in separate containers until ready for use. Since B is flammable, the solution should be stored in an airtight container, such as a 20-mm ammunition box. A polyethylene bag, sawdust and a baby syringe are useful to carry out the rest of the procedure. Depending on the particular situation, one may decide to pour NG into the desensitizer or sawdust or to pour the desensitizer or sawdust into the NG. When sawdust is used, the technician is actually making dynamite, which is less sensitive to shock than NG. The baby syringe is used to inject the solution into a safe if the safe is loaded with nitroglycerine.

Figure 133. An involved citizen pointing to the spot where he found a booster bomb. The bomber had tried to throw it through the second-story window, shown above the officer's head.

Figure 134. This is the same misfired booster bomb shown in Figure 133. The finder carried it into the office of the apartment building, and the police carried it to their station.

Washing down a safe or bank vault door is difficult because nitroglycerine will seep into narrow cracks and screw threads. About 1960, in Canada, a safe had been washed down extensively, but when the

Figure 135. This safe was opened with a very neat dial shot. None of the contents of the safe were damaged when the door was opened with a small amount of explosives.

safe mechanic later turned a screw, NG in the threads exploded, causing minor injuries to the mechanic. In a Miami Beach case (Fig. 137), burglars exploded three shots of NG in an eight-inch-thick steel vault door, and they left a fourth shot due to a faulty fuse. (The fuse had been last made in the United States in 1934 and last made in Mexico in 1954; the year was 1969.) The bomb technician washed down the door, which had NG in cracks left by the previous blasts, and dismantled the door, following directions of the safe mechanic (Fig. 138). A word of caution on the use of the desensitizer solution: it will eat the skin off your hands and has a disagreeable odor.

Figure 139 is a photograph of a fascinating demonstration of nitro-glycerine being improvised. This procedure is not recommended unless the maker has the high degree of knowledge and experience of Gerd Ester.

Figure 136. The author took this photograph of an actual bottle of nitroglycerine that was completely maroon in color.

Binary Explosives

Binary explosives are those materials that are sold in two parts and do not become explosives until they are mixed before they are used, usually at a job site. They were developed as a result of rocket research. Astrolite was the first such explosive that became commercially available, but supposedly, Astrolite is no longer manufactured. Astrolite becomes pure liquid when it is mixed by the user and in that form developed the same velocity of detonation as nitroglycerine or C4.

Kinetics was the second commercial company to produce a binary explosive. It has become more widely used. Binary materials do not require rigid laws of transportation and storage of explosive. Binary explosives require detonators for initiation which are restricted to high explosives regulations. Two-part binary explosives have become more popular and a third manufacturer now has an even more improved product.

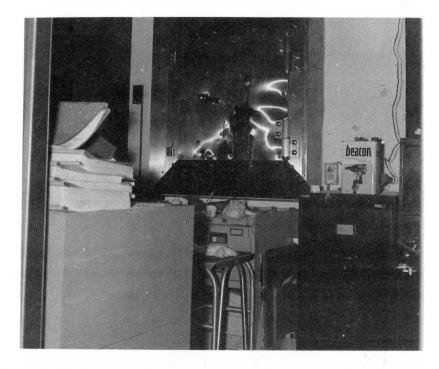

Figure 137. A bomb technician must be very careful and very thorough when removing and desensitizing nitroglycerine in a situation like this. Proper equipment should be available or a worse condition could develop.

Military Ordnance

Since World War II, there has been an enormous increase in new types of munitions, or military explosive ordnance. Most of the World War II ordnance that was used by Germany against England has been deactivated. However, in Germany, Belgium, France and nearby countries huge quantities of military ordnance from not only World War II but from World War I are still being destroyed. Figure 140 displays part of a live reference collection in Germany. Approximately 450 tons of munitions are being recovered and destroyed in Germany every year by the bomb squads of the public works departments of the individual German states as shown in Figure 141. Explosive ordnance, in the form of mines, artillery shells, aerial bombs, small arms ammunition and a wide variety of related items are being found underground and underwater every day. Belgium disposes of 400 tons of explosive ordnance every year. France recovers and destroys 900 tons of dangerous ordnance yearly.

Figure 138. Dismantling the inside of this vault door loaded with nitroglycerine was one of the most dangerous jobs the author ever had to undertake.

Figure 139. Gerd Ester demonstrating the improvisation of nitroglycerine with the assistance of the author. Photograph courtesy of Steve Brodie.

Many more countries manufacture and sell military ordnance. Ordnance is stockpiled or stored and, as technology improves, new models replace the old material which is valuable and rarely destroyed. Intelligence information has shown that some countries that have large military forces but where they may be in financial difficulty, these countries have resorted to selling ordnance for food. Drug dealers, criminals of all sorts, terrorists and revolutionists are using and scattering military ordnance throughout the world.

The United States and most foreign military ordnance have render safe procedures (RSP), but some foreign ordnance do not. The land mines that have been scattered in war zones and restricted areas of socialist countries have been supplemented by the scattering of mini-mines. Mini-mines are submunitions that are scattered from a larger container dropped from aircraft or deployed by artillery rounds. Many submunitions have an innocuous appearance and constitute an enormous problem to civilian populations where they have been used in wartime. Some submunitions are extremely sensitive to movement or pressure.

Figure 140. Gerd Ester providing information to former East German bomb squads on a live reference collection of military ordnance.

Figure 141. Tons of live military ordnance like this are being disposed of everyday in European countries. The Franco-Prussian War, WW I and WW II make bomb disposal a hazardous occupation for many people and inhabitants.

Anyone who responds to a request for disposal of military ordnance should identify it correctly before touching it. Some military ordnance can be identified by color coding or by nomenclature marked on its container. The next step is to determine if it is armed or safe. Some items can be handled in either condition, while others are extremely sensitive to initiation in an armed condition. Some ordnance may be marked "armed" or "safe," while other ordnance may have no markings.

Some float flares recovered in South Florida may burn after being removed from the water and dried. Some float flares, that are recovered, may begin to burn after being immersed in water again. These flares are hazardous to carry in patrol cars or to store in magazines with explosives. Unless an isolated storage area is available, the best procedure is to take supposedly used float flares to a disposal site for demolition. Reworked military ordnance, or improvised explosive devices of any sort, cannot be trusted to function in the method that the original manufacturer or the modifier intended. Remote methods of initiation or partial testing of modified systems with backup demolition charges may be advisable when disposing of recovered military ordnance. Many of the 4,000 bombs that the author disposed of were forms of military ordnance from terrorists.

Veterans of military service who work in the police or fire department may attempt to handle the ordnance themselves. Frequently they incorrectly identify it. One fire department in South Florida received a grenade and, not knowing whether it was live, handled it around the office for a week. Finally they took it out to the woods, pulled the pin and threw it into a canal, where it exploded.

Unless you are familiar with the ordnance, then the best course is to call the closest EOD team. There are so many types of ordnances that EOD personnel from one branch of the service do not recognize all the ordnance from the other branches. Military field-training manuals should be carried in the bomb truck to help in the recognition of different ordnance.

Color codes and markings on ordnance cannot be trusted. Revolutionary groups frequently rework and reload ordnance with their own explosives and initiating devices. However, markings, nomenclature and numbers on ordnance should be recorded before it is destroyed (Fig. 142).

If a person does not know the ordnance, he should not trust it to

Figure 142. Shown are eighteen blue sand-and-water filled practice bombs which were loaded by Cuban exiles with 30 pounds of dynamite in each along with a homemade impact nose. The author dismantled them, following the bomb-maker's precautions.

perform in its original manner. Trying to throw grenades while expecting a time delay may result in a surprise for the technician. A member of the New York Police Bomb Squad had his hand severely mangled by a grenade with a bad fuse.

The United States Armed Forces Explosive Ordnance Disposal personnel have the responsibility of first response to atomic or nuclear device incidents. Nuclear Emergency Search Teams (NEST), under the Department of Energy, have the ultimate responsibility of dealing with anything suspected of being an atomic or nuclear weapon.

COMMERCIAL EXPLOSIVES AND
MILITARY ORDNANCE CHECKLIST

The following steps are a guide and will vary with the individual situation.

Upon Arrival

1. Contact officer or complainant for information on item.

Examination of Item

1. Without touching, notice shape, color, size and markings for determination of type of explosive.
2. If the item cannot be identified, consult Sax's *Handbook of Dangerous Industrial Materials* or military ordnance field manuals.
3. If military ordnance type is unknown, telephone Army or Navy Explosive Ordnance Disposal Unit (depending on type of ordnance) for assistance in disposal or advice.
4. Contact the Bureau of Alcohol, Tobacco and Firearms (1-800-800-3855) to identify commercial explosives or military ordnance and trace it to determine if it is stolen.

Fuse Information

1. Note core color, insulation color, length, wrapper markings and serial number.
2. Preserve wrapper for fingerprints if necessary.
3. Photograph item along with ruler to show size.
4. Place in magazine for future disposal.

Detonating Cord Information

1. Note core color, insulation color, length, spool or box markings and serial number.
2. Preserve spool or box for fingerprints if necessary.
3. Photograph item with ruler.
4. Place in dynamite magazine for future disposal.

Cap Information

1. Note color of cap, and color of writing, color of interior of fuse caps, length of cap, whether it has round, flat or dimple end, number and type of crimps on electric caps, color of plug, color of wires, length of wires, type of shunt, writing on delay tag or sleeve, and size, color, writing, serial number on box.
2. Photograph items along with ruler.
3. Place cap in magazine for future disposal.

Dynamite, Emulsions, ANFO or Blasting Agents

1. Note color of cartridge, box and writing, writing and number of cartridges and boxes, length and diameter of cartridge and box, number of cartridges and boxes, color and consistency of filler

explosive, whether there is a liner in box and the approximate condition of the box—new, old or leaking.
2. Photograph item with ruler.
3. Place dynamite in magazine for future disposal.
4. Acetone is the universal solvent for all explosives, except black powder. The solvent for black powder is water.

Nitroglycerine

1. Mix solution A with solution B.
2. Pour desensitizer into nitroglycerine or pour nitroglycerine into desensitizer.
3. Pour sawdust into nitroglycerine or pour nitroglycerine into sawdust.

Chapter 10

EVIDENCE OF EXPLOSIVES

DEFINITION OF A BOMB

A criminal bomb is an explosive substance which is placed, dropped, thrown or projected with the unlawful intention of causing either injury, death, or destruction of property, or creating a disturbance (Figs. 143 and 144). When a bomb is put at a scene by one of the above methods, it is called "planting" or "setting." If the item in question is a letter bomb or package bomb, delivery is still by means of being placed, dropped, thrown or projected. A bomb may be used to coerce or intimidate others. Every bombing ordinarily has a meaning or message to the person for whom it is intended. It is, however, difficult to determine motive or reasons for some bombings (Fig. 145).

REASONS FOR BOMBING

One Cuban bomber in Miami, who became angry over two misfortunes that happened to him in one day, got mad at the world. He collected 32 sticks of dynamite from his closet and drove around until he found a place to put them. He blew up a tree in the middle of a city park. Windows were broken in almost every house around the block (Fig. 146).

Frequently the victim is reluctant to tell, or will not tell, the authorities the reason for the bombing. The person who tells the police that he does not have the slightest idea why anyone would bomb him or that he does not have an enemy in the world is usually hiding information. One Miami Beach victim of a bomb hoax gave this standard statement to the police after a shoebox containing a clock, batteries and caulking compound similar to C4 in appearance was dismantled. A note enclosed in the box told the victim, "You have 24 hours to pay up." A veteran police officer knew the complainant was a bookie who must have followed instructions later, since he never received any real bombs afterwards (Fig. 147). So a background check and skillful interview may bring out many reasons for the bombing.

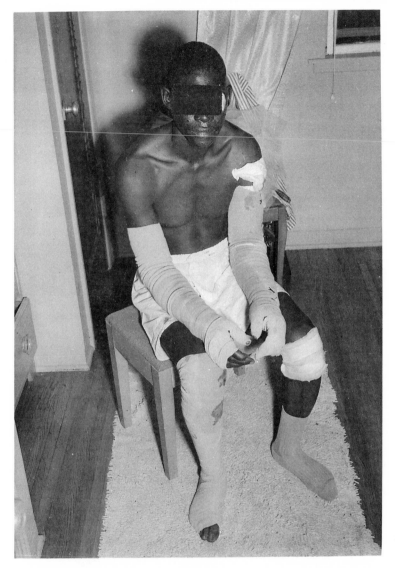

Figure 143. The victim of a package bomb who was fortunate that he lived. Package bombs are usually booby trapped to cause death or injury. Package bombs usually leave much more evidence to assist in tracing down the bomber or for his conviction.

If the victim is killed in a bombing, he obviously will not be able to comply with an intimidation. Since most of the bombings in Dade County and the rest of the country have been for intimidation, they usually have been time bombs. For death or injury, many bombs are set off by some movement of the victim. Command-initiated bombs are used for pinpointing targets. Therefore, there may be many bomb scares,

Figure 144. Fragments are shown of the package bomb that injured the victim in the previous figure. Pieces of board and paper matched those in the suspect's vehicle.

Figure 145. The entire building of the Democratic Executive Committee was destroyed in this bombing in Miami which was two blocks south of federal and local government buildings, shown at the top of the photograph.

Figure 146. A reliable informant advised the author of the identify of the bomber responsible for this incident. We could not ascertain any motive, until that information was received.

bomb hoaxes or small bombs exploded without the intention of causing injury or death (Fig. 148). The victim often realizes this and knows that unless he complies, he or his family may be killed by another bomb. A loan shark in Miami had both legs blown off when his car exploded but still would not talk because of the possibility of further retaliation against him or his family.

INVESTIGATION

As in most criminal investigations, the victim is a possible suspect. His family, friends and associates also must be eliminated as suspects in a bombing investigation (Fig. 149). A Cuban exile in Miami bombed his own property several times for publicity for his revolutionary cause.

Figure 147. The author carefully deactivated this partly open package bomb, only to find that instead of C4, it contained caulking compound. If real explosives had been used, the bomber may have killed himself, since the circuit was wired incorrectly.

Purpose of an Investigation

The purpose of an explosion or bombing investigation is to determine what was the cause of the incident so that future incidents can be avoided. The events and situations leading up to the time of the incident and the resulting effects are all observed as completely as possible. The incident may have been criminal or accidental.

The majority of bombing cases are solved through evidence given by informants. After the identity of a bomber is discovered, it often takes time to develop incriminating evidence without entrapment. A community may have a series of bombings perpetrated by only one person or a small group. Once that particular group is apprehended, the bombing will cease abruptly. As in all violations of the law, if a person feels he will not be caught, he may try to get away with it. The success of one bomber may cause others to get the idea. It is a big deterrent when a group is apprehended (Figs. 150, 151, and 152).

Figure 148. The front and rear doors were locked prior to this bomb explosion. All of the windows were intact. This was a union headquarters in which the local was being sued and the labor department was after their records. Allegedly, the records were destroyed, but they were not.

Infiltration of groups by police informants is risky, and attempting to find the right type of person to enter such a closely knit group may be nearly impossible. One Cuban organization had the following precautions. Only the leader knew all the facets of the plan; false information was given to different members to try to locate spies; members changed cars when traveling and had one car follow another to ward off tails. Yet, members of this group were arrested five times and finally convicted.

In several investigations and arrests, detectives have found that a bomb disposal technician may be helpful in interviews of witnesses or interrogations of suspects. The author has been able to establish a rapport with bombers and witnesses simply through praise of a cause or admiration of a bomb's workmanship. Bombers are proud of their work and some of them are anxious to brag. The information obtained from them is helpful in obtaining more evidence and in future investigations.

Most bombing investigations today are done through the joint efforts of many different local, state and federal agencies. Cooperation and

Figure 149. This bomber was called, "The White Hand." Cuban Power claimed credit, however, and collected $10,000. A white workman's glove, a time pencil and pieces of dynamite wrapper were found at the scene.

mutual sharing of information necessitates meetings in which teams are organized and tasks are delegated. Communications between agencies should be established before bombing incidents occur so decisions as to lines of authority and responsibility are not debatable in emergencies.

The Federal Bureau of Investigation, the Bureau of Alcohol, Tobacco and Firearms and the Postal Department are willing and able to furnish investigators, equipment, and laboratory facilities both inside and outside the United States. Bombing investigations have had an enormous increase in trained bomb scene investigators in the last twenty years.

Scene Preservation

As in a case where an unexploded bomb has been found, it is necessary to search the scene of an exploded bomb for a second unexploded one as shown in Figure 153. This is different from a "secondary device," which is a second bomb intended to kill or injure rescue, bomb disposal or other official personnel or civilians. A secondary initiating system may

Figure 150. The stern of this ship was sunk in the Port of Miami by a Cuban Power group. This was the fourth in a series of ship sinkings which came close to killing innocent citizens of several countries, including the United Kingdom, Spain, Mexico and Japan.

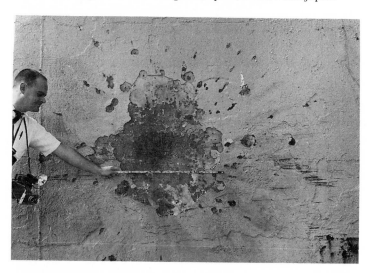

Figure 151. A bomb caused this dent in the side of a Polish ship in the Port of Miami. This was the last attack by Cuban Power before their apprehension. Approximately 80 percent of the fragments from a 57-mm recoilless HEAT round were recovered by dragging a magnet at a 45-degree angle along the harbor bottom.

be an additional safety or a booby trap. This is especially true today, since revolutionary groups might want to kill police officers and fire fighters in an attempt to overthrow the government. The first small bomb may be exploded in order to get an officer to the scene where a

Figure 152. This Chinese recoilless 57-mm rifle, shell canister and expended shell were found in the water at the point of attack 200 yards from the Polish ship.

larger bomb (time, remote control or motion activated) has been left to cause injury or death.

Rescue of injured or trapped survivors is the first consideration at any explosion scene. If there are no injuries or fire danger, the police and fire fighters should clear the area, both to preserve evidence and to protect lives. The bomb technician should search the scene for other bombs. A good distance for scene preservation with most bombs is 300 feet from the center, but fragments may go even farther. Fragments from one car bombing in Miami were found 600 feet from the car and some had gone through the roof of a three-story building. In brief, the outer limits of scene preservation should be where the piece of fragmentation farthest from the center of the explosion is found. In one huge explosion in Dade County, windows were broken five miles from the center. Fragments of the truck involved were found one-half mile from the crater (Fig. 154).

Safety equipment for rescue personnel and post-blast-scene-search personnel consists of gloves, clothing, hard hats, steel-toe shoes, breathing apparatus, goggles, and ear muffs, depending upon the conditions.

Figure 153. This bombing occurred in a men's room trash can in the states attorney's office after the subject called a local TV station the night before, stating he would do it. Within 24 hours the subject did six other bombings of public buildings.

Falling debris, broken glass and live wires are just a few of the unsafe conditions at bombing scenes. Lighting is a common problem, since most bombings occur at night and fragile lights are easily broken by bomb blasts.

Police officers often forget to look for fingerprints at bombing scenes. Possible entrances and exits should also be searched for shoe and tire impressions as well as for signs of forced entry. Fingerprints, tool impressions and fracture patterns are the most common forms of positive identification on bombing investigations.

Need for Physical Evidence

Thorough investigation of evidence can develop valuable leads. The questions which are often asked by investigators and top brass are, What type of explosive was it and how much was used? The answer can be given immediately if the explosive fails to explode fully. The military terminology is to "low order" (Fig. 155). The reason for this is that there were either defective explosives or inadequate priming (Figs. 156 and 157).

UNEXPLODED EXPLOSIVES

In a dynamite explosion, the paper and the wax are carbonaceous fuel which is balanced with oxygen by the manufacturers, so that it should all be consumed in the explosion. However, the oxidizing salts in the dynamite are hygroscopic, similar to table salt. These salts will pick up moisture from the air and ruin the initiation sensitivity of the dynamite. The individual sticks are sealed in wax to prevent this, but improper storage in a humid atmosphere and opening or breaking of the cartridges will cause the breakdown of dynamite. Pieces of wet dynamite and paper will be found in the bottom of the crater or scattered around the area only in rare cases. The bombing in Figure 158 is an excellent example.

Composition "C" plastic explosive requires an engineer's special blasting cap surrounded at the base end by the explosive to insure detonation. Smaller caps improperly placed will result in misfires and scattering of all or part of the composition explosive as seen in Figure 159. Figure 160 is an excellent example of a high-velocity explosion.

Figure 154. A trailer containing 17,000 pounds of dynamite exploded after thieves set it on fire to ruin their fingerprints. Fifty feet from the crater, the tire iron and a padlock were found. Another similar incident in which 22,000 pounds exploded blew three youths to smithereens.

The Lidstone Cartridge Test

Don Lidstone developed this method of examining small amounts of suspected explosive material while working at Woolwich Arsenal in the United Kingdom. Test results as shown in Figure 161 not only determine if the substance is explosive but will also disclose its approximate velocity. Approximately three-eighths of an inch of the material is packed into the bottom of a .303 Enfield cartridge and a number six electric detonator or blasting cap is inserted in the end of the cartridge. The cartridge is placed in a steel cylinder approximately one foot by two feet in height

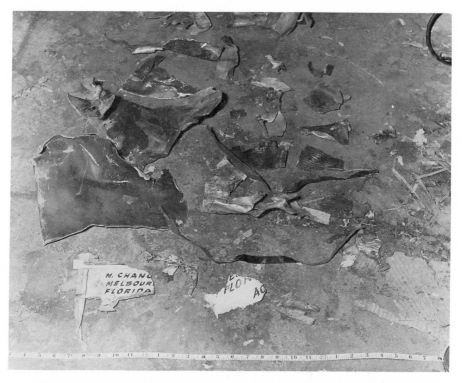

Figure 155. This package bomb in Haiti left many fragments of the container and the outside shipping container. There were two bombs on the same Pan American flight.

Figure 156. One bomber lost his hand when he attempted to explode a misfired bomb with a smokeless, powder-loaded grenade. Arrow 1 is a finger, 2 is the center of the explosion which scattered unburned smokeless powder and 3 is a second grenade dropped at the scene by the bombers.

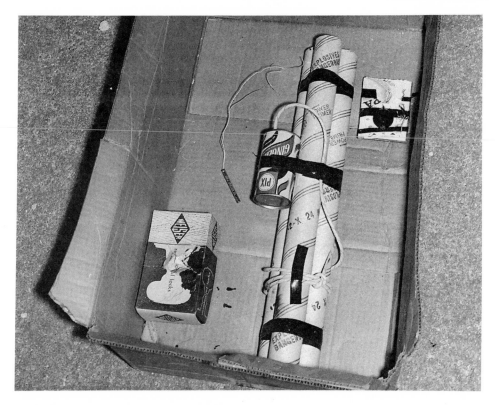

Figure 157. Shown here is a 10-pound dynamite bomb which misfired and the author dismantled and disposed of.

which is partially filled with vermiculite. The cylinder is closed and the cap initiated. The contents of the cylinder are sifted and the base of the cartridge is examined. The test may be performed inside laboratories and is quite safe. The displayed results show the same differences in velocities of black powder, dynamite, TNT and plastic explosive. Don Lidstone's test results have been accepted in British courts.

If an individual is tried for the possession of explosives without a permit, this type of test may be all that is necessary to prove the material in question is explosive. Chemical analysis will verify composition of the material. Both tests will reinforce each other in court.

MISFIRES

The main reasons for misfires with fuse caps are either a faulty crimp of the cap to the fuse as shown in Figure 162 or the use of fuse ends that

Figure 158. Pieces of fuse, tape, and dynamite wrapper were found pasted to floor tile in the bottom of a crater. Dynamite wrappers should only be found if the dynamite has absorbed too much moisture from the atmosphere or is improperly primed.

have become moist. Some nervous bombers will fail to ignite the fuse. If one wrap of a coil of fuse is in contact with a second wrap, the heat is transferred to the second wrap or section of the fuse, and this heat may melt the asphalt insulation, causing it to cut off the powder train in the second section. When the fuse burns down to this section, it may go out. Kinked fuse may interrupt the powder train and when the fire reaches this spot, the fiber may burn slowly until it reaches powder again. Everyone who has played with firecrackers as a child will remember this from misfires with the paper fuse of firecrackers which possibly exploded when they were picked up again. Another reason for misfires with fuses is improper ignition with fuse lighters. A bomber who is in a hurry may pull a fuse lighter and then throw the bomb without making sure the fuse is burning. This happened in Fort Lauderdale where the bomber was not familiar with the type of fuse lighter.

The main reason for misfires with electric caps is faulty wiring connections or dead batteries. This type of bomb is difficult to deactivate. The main reason for misfires with time pencils is insufficient pressure applied to break the glass vial of copper sulfate.

Figure 159. This C4 bomb "low ordered" splattering C4 around the area when the blasting cap was initiated. The bomb had been delivered by dropping it through the mail slot in the door which was a common means of entry for bombs.

Figure 160. This C4 book bomb detonated prematurely as the bomb makers were putting it together. Fragments of hands and the bomb penetrated this nearby door.

Figure 161. The Lidstone cartridge explosive test. A cartridge on the left is exploded with a small sample of suspected explosive initiated by a number 6 blasting cap. The results always duplicate. From left to right are inert dirt, black powder, dynamite, TNT and C4. The results prove that the material is explosive and its relative burning rates.

GAS EXPLOSIONS

The type and amount of explosive can be estimated by the type and amount of damage (Fig. 163). A big question to determine is whether an explosion was caused by gas or a bomb. A low-velocity explosion is characterized by pushing effects on persons and objects. A gas explosion is low velocity.

A mixture ratio of 1.4 percent to 7.6 percent gasoline to air is an explosive mixture. A mixture of 4.5 percent gasoline to air gives the best explosive effects. Less than 1.4 percent will not explode, but more than 7.6 percent can be spread to better proportions for burning or exploding. You can see that this percentage of fuel is very low. This is the reason an equal weight of gasoline will produce more explosive force than an equal weight of dynamite (Fig. 164). Dust or flour explosives are similar to gas explosives in effects and principle.

Figure 162. A faulty crimp let this bomb lay on a rooftop for months before it was discovered. The author pulled the cap from the dynamite prior to the photograph.

The two main things the investigator of a gas vapor explosion is seeking are the source of the gas leak and the source of the ignition. The type of gas, how much and how long it leaked into the atmosphere may be learned through interview of victims and witnesses, examination of containers, pipes, fittings, labels, receipts, manometer and chemical analysis. Determination if damage was done to gas fixtures before, during or after explosions may be done by a metallurgist.

Gas vapors will continue to accumulate and spread until it is either ignited or it is dissipated. If you are fortunate, the wind will dissipate it, or you may be able to hose down the area with water before the gas is ignited as seen in Figure 165. Whether the gas is lighter or heavier than air is one of the first facts to determine. Gas going into cracks and crevices may create problems in dispersing it or it may show in explosion effects typical of that type of gas.

At a gasoline refinery explosion in Venezuela, which the author investigated, gas vapors spread over an area of 200 yards before they exploded as shown in Figure 166. The effects of this interesting explo-

Figure 163. Remains from a typical gas-vapor explosion. The greatest effects are found where the gas-to-air proportions are properly balanced.

sion showed a classic example of a gas explosion. Seven lives were lost and damage was in the millions of dollars.

At an explosion scene, gas vapors will collect in different areas due to wind and confinement in structures. This will cause inconsistencies in effects and propagation of the explosion wave.

Figures 167 and 168 depict the effects of a crankcase explosion of a diesel engine which initiated a devastating boiler explosion on a ship. The author worked in conjunction with marine architects in the examination of a sister ship and blueprints were used to reconstruct events. A week prior to the disaster a crankcase explosion had occurred on the ship, but no one realized exactly what it was. A thorough investigation may have found the cause and prevented the catastrophe.

Victims of gas explosions are frequently burned all over, except where shoes protect their feet. Often they may live for short periods of time. During this time, they may at first be in shock and difficult to interrogate. A victim may not be able to speak because the inside of his mouth is burned. When such a person has been treated with painkilling drugs, it is hard to obtain coherent stories from him. Cruel as it may seem, some

Figure 164. In this case of arson with gasoline, the explosion of the vapors blew the front window 200 feet away. When a business blows up and burns at night, arson can be suspected. This business was involved in labor difficulties. Frequently, explosions and fires are perpetrated by the owners.

valuable information may be obtained by interview of the suffering victim in an attempt to solve the mystery of the cause of the explosion as shown in Figure 169. It is the investigator's duty to prevent more explosions of this type in the future or to determine if there is any civil or criminal liability to be decided by a court of law as seen in Figure 170. It is also his responsibility to the victim, his family, associates and the community to exhaust every possible source of information.

A person in a gas explosion, or at a distance from a high-velocity explosion, may not be injured at all, or he may be blown through a wall by the pushing effects of an explosion but without being burned as is illustrated in Figure 171. There are two reasons for this. First, from the point of initiation, it takes a period of space and time for the explosive wave or pressure to reach its peak. Second, the percentage of air-gas mixture might not be correct in the place where the victim is. In a room with the proper air-gas mixture, one wall might be blown out, yet small items in the room may be left untouched. After an explosion, examina-

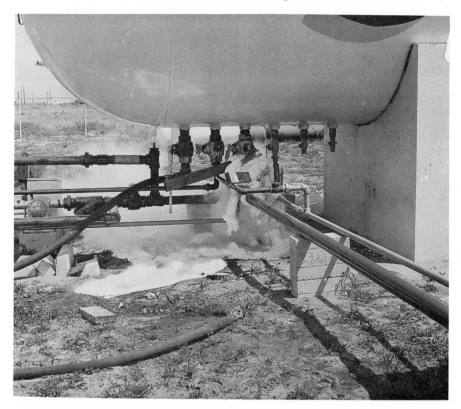

Figure 165. A bomb blew off pipe but failed to ignite the gas which froze after it was plugged. A fire truck responding to the scene was engulfed in fumes, but fortunately the gas was not ignited.

tion of an unburned area of the scene may disclose the smell of gas in a place to which the explosive wave did not reach, since there was not any more leakage of gas.

A relatively inexpensive portable explosive meter is good to verify what your nose tells you is probably an explosive gas-air mixture, but this meter does not tell you the type of fuel present. An experienced person may be able to testify in court that in his opinion, his sense of smell indicated a certain type of fuel. Some dogs have been trained to detect hydrocarbons at explosion scenes.

It is best to utilize a gas vacuum collection tube prepared at the laboratory to collect air samples from where the odor is strongest. If a collection tube is not available, a soft-drink bottle washed out with water may be filled with water. This is then poured out at the collection point, which will result in the fumes being sucked into the bottle. The bottle is

Figure 166. Exploding gasoline vapors surrounding this metal stretcher container squeezed the container from all sides like a giant hand. The vapors had been spread from the sweetening plant in the background at this refinery and ignited at the cracking plant where the author took the photograph.

capped and taken to the laboratory for analysis on a gas chromatograph. Porous material containing flammables should be transported to the laboratory in new, clean paint cans or jars. Polyethylene bags will allow the fumes to escape.

Gaseous vapor explosions are sometimes characterized by immediate ignition and burning afterwards of tinder, such as paper and fiber. There may be a big ball of flame in the explosion which subsides and is followed by subsequent burning. An explosion destroys a lot of evidence, but an explosion followed by a fire makes the investigation even more difficult. If you are lucky, paper and other tinder may be singed, but less flammable objects such as painted surfaces may or may not show the result of the heat.

A good indication of a gas explosion where gas had accumulated inside a partitioned wall is that during the explosion each side of the wall will go in different directions. Collapsing of sealed metal cans equally on all sides, similar to being squeezed by a giant hand, indicates the explosion of gas vapor on all sides.

Figure 167. The entire top deck and smokestack were blown off this large freighter and landed in the ocean. The boiler, which exploded, was in the center of the broken and twisted steel girders shown in the center of the photograph. Photograph courtesy of Steve Brodie.

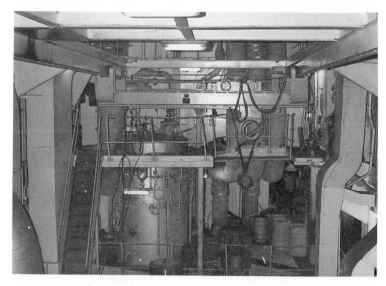

Figure 168. Fortunately, the sister ship was in port at the time of the examination which allowed this picture to be taken of the boiler as it had been before the disaster. Photograph courtesy of Steve Brodie.

Frequently in attempted arson, gasoline is poured throughout the building. The evaporating gasoline causes the building to become a gigantic bomb that explodes when the arsonist sets a match to it. The

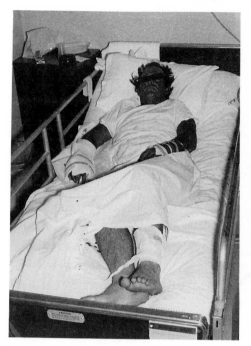 

Figure 169. (*Left*) Live victims of explosions and bombings should be interviewed as soon as possible after the incident, in case they expire. Doctors, hospital personnel, and paramedics should be interviewed and consulted concerning proper medical attention for explosion effects.

Figure 170. (*Right*) Clothing of victims of explosions and bombings should be collected and properly receipted before they may be destroyed. X-rays to show embedded fragments and photographs of wounds and bandages may be helpful.

effects can blow a concrete-block building apart. It may also save the state the cost of prosecution, as in the following example shown in Figure 172. One arsonist in Sanford, Florida was blown through a wall and the building fell on top of him when he ignited the contents of a five-gallon and a two-gallon can of gasoline, which he had poured throughout the premises. Parts of the walls were blown 200 feet.

Gasoline is difficult to ignite in dynamite explosions, unless the explosion is initiated in the fumes above the surface of the liquid. Black powder will ignite gasoline easily. This may be noted in the next modern war movie you see when the ground burns after an explosion because they used gasoline to highlight the explosion. High-velocity explosives by themselves do not leave the ground burning afterwards. C4 also will ignite gasoline better than dynamite. Dynamite exploded inside the passenger compartment of an automobile causes the fiber or upholstery

Figure 171. A gas explosion blew this wall out. Questioning of victims before they died assisted in the reconstruction of events.

to smolder and eventually catch fire as in Figure 173, but C4 will ignite upholstery instantaneously.

There have been two bombings of liquid petroleum (LP) gas plants in Dade County. In one case, the LP gas was ignited, causing widespread destruction of the plant. Gas-storage cylinders have safety valves that supposedly melt in a fire, allowing the contents to escape and burn. In this first case, some gas burned and some exploded.

In the bombing, a four-inch pipe was blown off a large tank by a bomb. The occupants of the first fire truck at the scene found themselves in the midst of what they at first thought was ground fog. When the firemen saw from where the gas vapor was escaping, they turned off their engine ignition and radio and walked to a telephone to call for another truck to wash down the vapors.

A common occurrence in the burning of a hot material on a cement surface is the explosion of the cement. The moisture in the cement turns to steam, which explodes, causing a shallow, glassy, irregularly shaped crater with very gradually sloping sides and no cracks, depressions or pulverization of the bottom of the crater. This can occur with a gasoline-

Figure 172. In the examination of this gasoline vapor explosion and fire, it was necessary to remove the collapsed roof to disclose the vapor explosion effects on the refrigerator shown on the right. The burn pattern of the gasoline can be seen on the wood floorboards of the bar.

soaked rug on cement or with a burning of magnesium shavings on cement. These craters may be scattered, and an inexperienced investigator may take them for high-velocity explosion craters.

HIGH-VELOCITY EXPLOSIONS

An explosion scene investigation, as shown in Figure 174, whether it is an accidental explosion or a bombing scene, is now sometimes referred to as a post-blast investigation. The bombing investigator should bear in mind all of the reasons that are listed in Chapter 4 for bomb containers, different types of initiation and his knowledge of explosives. A thorough study of dismantled batteries, clocks and watches is a good background for recognizing possible bomb fragments.

Figure 173. A dynamite bomb on the front seat ignited the upholstery which smouldered until fire fighters extinguished it.

Cause and Effect

Cause-and-effect investigation shows that the chemical change in an explosive bomb is the cause. The bomb's initiation, the chemical change of the explosive, the heat, pressure, vacuum, and fragmentation of the bomb and the environment (including people) are all part of the explosion. All of the damage or anything that is caused to change is all the effect. In other words, the explosive does not explode. The explosive has a chemical change that is the cause. The scene explodes. The entire scene is the explosion which is the effect as seen in Figure 175.

A high-velocity explosion is characterized by a central shattering point with damage radiating outward in all directions from this point (Fig. 176). If the explosion occurs in midair, there will be no central crater, but there will be a radiation or sunburst pattern on property or objects surrounding the explosion center. Pushing effects similar to those of gas explosions are found farther away from this central point (Fig. 177). Victims are injured and property is damaged mainly on the

Figure 174. A states rights group did two series of bombings in Miami, including this one of the editor of *The Miami Herald.* A nine-year-old girl slept right through this explosion just outside her bedroom. A thread of time fuse was found embedded in a nearby tree.

side facing the center of the explosion. An explosion travels in a straight line and will go the path of least resistance, but it will not take the time to look for it.

The amount of heat, pressure and fragmentation produced by a bomb depends on the type, amount, quality, condition, configuration, confinement, density, contaminants, location and initiation of the bomb. Initiation, itself, depends upon the size, amount, direction and location of the initiator in relation to the bomb. Barriers provide protection, but the blast will sweep around corners and may reflect from a barrier, changing the direction of the force to go around corners with even more devastating effects. When explosion pressure deflects off a surface and hits pressure deflected off another surface, they reinforce each other. The total effects may be much more devastating. That is why inside corners of buildings become weak points when explosions occur inside rooms.

Although it is helpful to know the type of explosive used, circumstances vary the effects and it may even be hazardous to the investigation

Figure 175. The author is shown scraping fragments of a tape recorder off the wall of the hallway outside the homicide office of the Miami Police station. Even though the bomber had called and said he was going to bomb the station and it was searched twice and was still being searched at the time of the explosion, the unknown tape recorder was not examined.

to state only on the basis of effects, that a single type of explosive was used. A report may read, "The damage was caused by a bomb with effects equivalent to the detonation of one pound of composition C4 plastic explosive, but it could be any other type of high-velocity explosive."

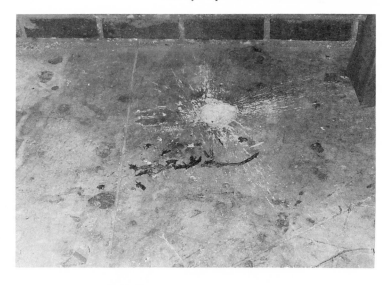

Figure 176. The radiation configuration emanating from the center of this crater may indicate the type and size of the container. Pieces of burned fuse were placed adjacent to the crater for this picture.

Figure 177. The author found pieces of the victim's fingers in all directions. The roof of the truck showed pieces of a battery splattered on the inside. The center of the explosion was about a foot above the floorboard of the truck. The owner had set a booby trap for a thief.

CRATERS

Craters may give a good indication of the type and quantity of explosive used (Figs. 178 and 179). Brisance refers to the shattering effect of the explosive. A high-velocity explosive has more shattering effect than a low-velocity explosive. Low-velocity explosives on dirt will make craters of wide diameter and shallow depth. High-velocity explosives will make craters of small diameter in relation to their depth. Low-velocity explosions will cause a crater with gradually sloping sides, and high-velocity-explosion craters will have steep sides (Fig. 180).

Figure 178. The author showing how to take a measurement of the depth of a crater.

On cement, low-velocity explosions make grooves and gouges from a metal container (Fig. 181). Unconfined low-velocity explosives may just leave discoloration on the surface. Cardboard or paper containers may be pasted to a cement surface by the explosion, leaving no crater at all (Fig. 182). Dynamite may depress cement and not remove any of it or very little of it. A dynamite crater may have concentric cracks in the cement surrounding the crater. C4 may leave no concentric cracks in the cement.

Dynamite on top of heavy steel may just discolor the metal or dent it. C4 will dent heavy steel, pit it or leave torn, jagged craters in it. C4 may cause small pieces of foreign material to strike metal, creating a

Figure 179. The author estimated approximately one pound of C4 was used to punch this hole in the concrete apron outside the garage door of the British Consul. A reliable informant advised us later that that was what the perpetrator used.

dimpling effect much larger than the fragmentation. Thin metal containers may be found welded or bonded to heavy steel in these pitted areas, similar to the explosive heat-pressure bonding manufacture of the silver and copper combination coins.

BLACK POWDER, DYNAMITE, C4, DETONATING CORD

Low-velocity explosions such as black powder and homemade mixtures of chemicals will require a compact container for confinement to make them explode instead of burn. Therefore, parts of a bomb container may indicate low-velocity explosive to increase the burning rate, although high-velocity explosives may be placed in containers for concealment or for shrapnel effect (Fig. 183). Confining the lower-velocity explosives in a container which is less than six inches in diameter will increase their velocity. For instance, at dynamite factories, sample explosion tests of batches are made constantly. Since dynamite is most commonly used in the ground, it is tested within a pipe to simulate its being underground. This will increase the velocity of detonation, for example, from 10,000 ft/sec to 12,000 ft/sec. Confinement of TNT or C4 will not increase the velocity of detonation. The smaller the fragments of the

Figure 180. This was the first bombing that the author examined. Approximately, 50 pounds of dynamite had been used to demolish this five-room house.

container, the higher the velocity of the explosion. A pipe may be merely split and turned inside out by a slow explosion (Fig. 184). Examination of four characteristics of the metal will indicate the velocity of the explosive. These are (a) number of fragments, (b) shape, (c) hardness and (d) size. Also, scratches or gouges at the edge of a crater will indicate a bomb container (Fig. 185).

Fragmentation

From the pressure, heat, fragmentation and vacuum effects of an explosion, material of all sorts may vaporize. Their chemical composition may be changed into other chemical elements, compounds or mixtures. All sorts of materials may be examined at bombing scenes: tape, rubber, fabric, metal, glass, plastic, cement, asphalt, wood, flesh, bone, hair, dirt, rock, and vegetation.

The smoke from a chemical explosion is steam. White smoke is pure steam and gray or black smoke contains carbon. Anything that is vapor-

Figure 181. In this metal box bomb, pieces of the box as well as nails enclosed within it went in all directions when it exploded on the left floorboard of the truck. The driver initiated the bomb when he pulled the door open.

Figure 182. Pieces of a cardboard container were found pasted to the cement by the explosion that occurred at this scene. A large soot stain approximately five feet in diameter is seen on the underside of the steps of this dormitory. The low-velocity blast blew off two doors adjacent to the stairwell.

ized may change from its physical state of solid, liquid or gas to steam. Larger fragments may be found as dust and even larger fragments found as granules. The vaporized items may condense on other parts of the

Figure 183. A pipe bomb filled with dynamite caused 75 holes in the side of this building and 25 holes in a truck across the street. The crater can be seen one foot to the left of the paper bag.

Figure 184. These large pieces of pipe were from a low-velocity black powder explosion at a university.

Figure 185. Grooves on the right side of the crater shown in this illustration were caused by fragments from a M26 grenade that was thrown into a restaurant.

environment, i.e. oxidation of metal caused by salts and steam. The dust may settle or adhere to other parts of the environment. The granules may be found to have struck other parts of the environment with such force that they are embedded into that object. Upon impact, a fragment may penetrate, adhere, reflect backwards, deflect in another direction, be disintegrated, leave a mark, drop to a surface below or be taken in another direction by vacuum or ricocheting pressure.

Several different things may happen to fragments. As they travel through the air or water their shape may change. They may break apart again into smaller fragments. Ricocheting pressure may change the direction of a moving fragment and the vacuum effect may move the fragment back toward the center of the explosion.

Holes may be found in objects at a scene but with little traces of what caused these holes. They may all be part of the pressure, ricocheting pressure or vacuum effects. Small holes of varying sizes may be found in plaster walls for instance, yet nothing is found inside the wall. An object may have struck the wall and disintegrated on impact as well as disintegrating that area of the wall. Careful microscopic or chemical analysis of the edges of the hole may reveal what struck it.

Several factors determine what happens to objects that come into contact with each other which are: size, weight, shape, composition, temperature, velocity, direction of travel, before and after impact and atmospheric conditions.

Sometimes the hole is smaller or larger than the fragment that strikes it. For example, at one scene where two perpetrators were making a booby-trap book bomb to send to someone else, the bomb exploded. A section of one of the perpetrator's hand, three inches in diameter, went through a one-inch hole in a plywood door. Conversely, a small half-inch steel fragment at high velocity may strike a head so hard that it makes a five-inch hole in the skull.

Some material, when it is fragmented, may do so in irregular sizes, depending on the nearness of the explosive and the direction from the explosive. For example, a pipe bomb may explode into little pieces, but the entire side of the pipe may be lying in the bottom of a crater where it was reinforced by an asphalt surface.

A study of the lines of force radiating from the center of the explosion will help locate the center of the explosion and will help locate fragments of the bomb. Using string or thin rods to follow holes that have been made in walls or other backstops will depict these lines of force. The radiation pattern may then be shown through photographs, measurements and drawings to help prove that a fragment was part of a bomb or that the bomb was adjacent to the fragment. Walls or other backstops act as witness plates that show the effects of the explosion and also as fragment catchers. It is not uncommon for single fragments to penetrate several walls or fragments. The depth of penetration of a fragment into a wall or medium may help a metallurgist estimate the burning rate of the explosive material. An experienced bomb scene investigator may give estimates but should allow for variances.

Fragments of metal from a low-velocity explosion may be stretched and bent along the edges, perhaps as thin and sharp as a knife. The heat and pressure from a C4 explosion will cause steel containers to turn blue-black.

In the examination of the scene, if elongated scratches, gouges or holes are found at the edge of the crater and holes are found driven into surrounding objects, there is a strong possibility that the explosive material had been in a container which was then turned into shrapnel by the explosion (Fig. 186). Pieces of the bomb are called "primary fragmentation." Primary fragmentation of military aerial bombs may travel at 5,000 ft/sec. Secondary fragmentation may travel faster because it takes time and space for the detonation wave to build up to its maximum speed, similar to a bullet being fastest just as it leaves the barrel. All fragments should be examined to determine if they are primary or secondary.

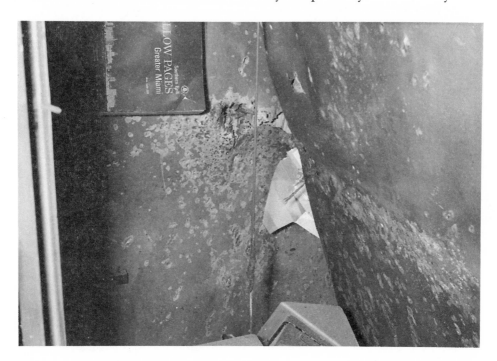

Figure 186. The position of the bomb scattered the shelf in this telephone booth upward. The bomb was a magnetic clam filled with C4 and initiated by a time pencil.

Pressure patterns, the dimensions of a crater, burn pattern, explosive residue patterns, odors, the color of smoke, the color and duration of flame, sound, implosion effects, the size and shape of fragments, the lines of force and penetration are all used by an experienced bomb scene or explosion scene investigator. This information is helpful in forming opinions, which should never be finalized prematurely. In some cases a conclusion may not be possible because not enough information is known or information is contradicting.

Sixteen Thousand Feet Per Second

The Battelle Corporation performed early research on pipe bomb fragments. Interesting phenomena occurs when an explosive burns above 16,000 fps. Any explosive that explodes this fast will not have its burning rate increased by confinement. Examination of steel that is subjected to an explosive that burns faster than 16,000 fps will disclose a "twinning" of the metal. Metal fragments are placed in a matrix by an examiner at the laboratory and polished. Under a low-power microscope small cracks, shaped like the letter "h," are apparent.

A good forensic laboratory technician or criminalist who is trained in metallurgy can be of great benefit in the examination of metal fragments from a bombing scene. Examination of metal may disclose if it was close to an explosion and if it was broken before or after an explosion. Wires, batteries, timing mechanisms and similar metals may be submitted to metallurgists for a complete examination.

A higher-velocity explosive will not cause pushing effects on objects at great distances or cause a large crater in proportion to the amount of explosive used. Its shattering effects are more complete on objects at the center of the explosion.

Windows broken a long distance from the scene indicate a slow or medium velocity. The exact position of an explosive in relation to the target or environment may greatly affect the results as shown in Figures 187 and 188. Several pounds of dynamite on top of a safe will cause little damage, but two ounces of dynamite inside the safe opens it easily.

A small crater in an area of dead leaves may be completely covered by leaves as a result of the vacuum phase of an explosion. The sudden outward air pressure is followed by equal but much slower movement of air pressure back again to refill the vacuum. This implosion will cause windows to break and objects behind barriers to move toward the center of the explosion but not in a straight line directly from the center. An example of this was a bomb exploding in an asphalt-paved parking lot behind a union hall in Miami. An eight-foot wall surrounded the lot, which helped the effect. Fifty feet away, broken windows were pulled thirty feet straight out to the south but not toward the crater, which was southeast of the windows.

Interrogation of witnesses may be of value in corroborating the results of the physical examination of the scene. A description of the type of sound heard may help. A sharp crack will indicate C4 or a bomb in the

Figure 187. The author is shown examining the center of an explosion in a meter room. This small amount of powerful explosive blew away the wall of the meter room and only made a small hole in the opposite wall.

Figure 188. The shock effect from the bomb in Figure 187 caused a spalling effect, throwing fragments of the wall throughout the room.

open. A dull thud or boom may indicate it was inside a building or it was a black-powder bomb. Often witnesses erroneously report repeated explosions which are, in fact, only echoes. An explosion on a quiet night will carry the sound of a small bomb for miles. Surrounding buildings, wind or the direction a person is facing may give false indications of the direction of an explosion. In several bombings, people in adjacent rooms or buildings have slept right through four-pound dynamite explosions. The idea is ridiculous, but witnesses will state that the explosion shook them out of bed when they live a mile from an explosion. Actually, the sound probably startled them so that they jumped out of bed and fell or they were merely exaggerating.

The color and size of the fireball of an explosion may indicate an incendiary mixed with the explosive. The color and amount of smoke can be important. Dynamite and black powder give white smoke. Smoke is merely steam. If the smoke is black or gray, this shows an excess of carbon, as seen in TNT or C4 explosions. Dirt and debris may be picked up by the explosion, but an astute observer will notice the debris and dirt drop, leaving the colored smoke to drift away.

Another ridiculous statement made by witnesses is that there was a smell of cordite at the scene. Cordite is a British propellant and has been dramatized in literature as the smell of fired cannons at battle scenes. If the explosion occurs outside in the wind, the odor of the explosion will not last as long as it will inside a building. If an explosion occurs inside, the smoke and odor will survive much longer. Dynamite explosions give a strong, sweet smell that lasts a long time. Military explosions give weak, acrid odors of short duration. Odors may prevail in wood, fabric or in dirt.

Exploded fireworks, black powder, smokeless powder, ANFO, dynamite, emulsions, TNT and RDX have different odors that some people can distinguish. In some cases where a whole building has been wrecked by a bomb, one may need his sense of smell to help him locate the center of the explosion where the smell is the strongest. In the last two decades electronic vapor detectors have been developed that not only can be used for bomb detection but also can be used for the examination of bombing scenes. A detector may be used to search for the center of an explosion and to help search for materials that may have been close to the center of the explosion including bomb fragments. At the laboratory the vapor detector may be used to examine containers of material from the bombing scene to determine which container is more likely to contain explosive residue. With luck the electronic vapor detector may distinguish which explosive may have been used in a bomb. Detectors with a small radioactive source are now the most sensitive machines used.

After the scene has been searched or while it is being searched for other bombs and witnesses are being questioned, photographs should be taken to show the relative effect of personal injury and property damage. A sketch should be made which will provide the necessary information about distances and the extent and type of damage represented by the photographs. Aerial photographs may help give a more complete picture of the damage.

Grid Pattern Search Method

The Bureau of Alcohol, Tobacco and Firearms has developed a grid pattern search method for collecting evidence in post-blast-scene investigations. The entire area that is to be searched is laid out in a grid pattern and all evidence that is collected is measured, photographed, marked and preserved in reference to the grid pattern. Any materials that are too small to be marked should be placed in marked and sealed containers.

The bomb technicians should search the entire area themselves. If the location covers a large area, an organized search party should be formed to conduct a thorough search. A team of six to eight men should comb the area, collecting all foreign, suspicious or unknown material. Any object which is definitely known to have come from the bomb should be photographed and measured before it is collected. Each man may carry an evidence bag in which he places all evidence he collects. The closer to the center of the explosion, the more likely that evidence will be found. The cross-hatch search plan has been found to be best for places where there is a large open area. This operates in the following way (Fig. 189). The search-party members must move in a straight line and keep abreast of each other. The bomb technician will follow a short distance behind the group and advise them on their findings, as well as controlling their movements. The pivot men (men on the end) will control the straightness of the forward movement. Fragments are often found on rooftops and near solid objects facing the explosion, from which they have ricocheted or dropped.

For thorough searches, it has been the experience of many agencies that searchers should walk through the same area in the opposite direction of the first crosshatch pattern. The searchers will see a different perspective from the different lighting angles.

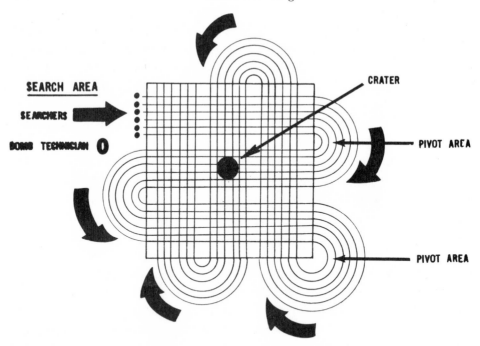

Figure 189. The crosshatch search pattern used for large outdoor areas will enable investigators to find the most evidence from a bombing. Retracing the same paths in the opposite direction may disclose evidence that was not seen in the first sweep of the area.

Measurements

Measurements of many different sorts may prove to be of value later. Besides the width, length and depth of the crater or seat of the explosion, measurements from the center of the crater to the respective pieces of evidence or bomb fragments may help. The distance between pieces of evidence or fragments and damage will help in estimates and description of effects. Two different points of reference from fixed objects will help place objects in scaled drawings later. Entrances, exits, viewpoints of witnesses and the closest person may help in an investigation. In court, it may be important for the prosecutor to show the closest area or building that people use to demonstrate the disregard for human life by the bomber(s).

Building and zoning, public works and traffic engineering departments are helpful in furnishing floor plans of buildings and scaled drawings and aerial photographs of bomb scenes. This information may be of assistance in investigations.

After a preliminary search, the best procedure is to collect all of the small debris by sweeping and shoveling it into large, clean garbage cans marked according to location. Later, back at the office, this debris is searched thoroughly by sifting it through progressively smaller screens.

In the search, every bit of debris must be examined and turned over piece by piece so the larger debris can be discarded at the scene. First, however, it must be examined for penetration of fragments of the bomb. In the center of the crater, the floor or ground may support or reinforce the bottom of a bomb container and prevent it from being completely disintegrated. Most of the time, the best evidence is not found in the crater but is found nearby where it has probably been stopped by barriers.

The shattered objects that are discolored by the explosion can be collected, and residues of the explosive or powdered, disintegrated material may sometimes be scraped off solid walls or metal adjacent to the explosion. In this case, it is necessary to carefully avoid scraping off paint or cement from the surface. A microscopic search of this matter may reveal minute particles of the bomb. A vacuum sweeper (electronic clue finder) can be used to go over the surrounding floor and wall to collect evidence that cannot be seen by the human naked eye.

Magnets

A magnet dragged through the crater and the immediate area around the crater may collect unseen evidence. Some searchers attach magnets to their gloves as they search or sift a scene. Magnets may be dragged or rolled over the entire scene using wheels on a bar magnet. The late Eddie Stone, a police technician with the Metro Dade Police Department, and his father developed an inexpensive electromagnet on wheels with a 12-volt battery that could be rolled over the scene like a lawnmower collecting fragments. When the switch is turned off, the iron or steel fragments drop onto an evidence-collection surface.

It should be remembered that a bomb must be delivered by being placed, dropped, thrown or projected, so searching of possible entrances and exits may give clues to the perpetrator (Fig. 190). In some cases, the bomber may have dropped pull wires or rings, matches, safety pins, cigarette butts or bomb parts at short distances from the scene or unconsciously left them in his pocket.

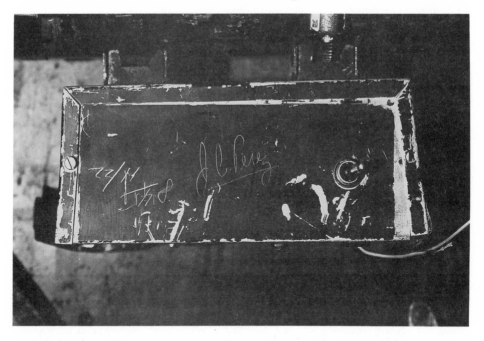

Figure 190. A bomb maker voluntarily autographed his improvised bazooka for Detective Al Gleason. This bomb maker left his *modus operandi* on bombings in Canada, New York, Florida and London.

In some instances, a line of black soot or tar is left when a fuse burns across a surface. Fuse gives off white smoke when it burns. In the investigation of an explosion, a mark or marks may be found on an adjacent wall where recently burned, hot fuse has ricocheted and left tar, fiber wrapping marks and evidence of the color of the fuse. Chemical analysis of these marks may confirm that it was fuse. The best surfaces from which to collect material for chemical analysis are any metal, wood or cement discolored by the explosion or by soot or burns that were adjacent to the explosion.

The bottom of the crater itself may be searched with fingers, sifted with different grades of mesh sieves and magnets and then collected in paint cans and the entire crater submitted to the laboratory for chemical analysis. Some chemists prefer that the crater not be searched first in order to prevent contamination.

After the crater and the immediate area surrounding the crater have been searched and collected, the floor or surface should be swept clean. Photographs may show possible heat, pressure, fragmentation, detonating cord or fuse patterns as shown in Figure 191.

Figure 191. Here, as indicated, are fragments of burned fuse embedded in a wood doorjamb. In other cases, burned fuse may strike with such force that it disintegrates and only leaves patterns at the impacted area.

An open-type bomb will leave less evidence than a closed-package bomb. Figure 192 depicts comparison evidence from labor-related bombings. Of course, if you can dismantle a bomb before it goes off or if it is a dud, you can save a lot of time searching the area for fragments. Just remember that your life is more important than evidence. If dynamite is used in the bomb, either a commercial or homemade electric blasting cap or fuse cap must be used to detonate it, in which case either wires or fuse may be found at the scene. In some areas, homemade caps have been used in bombings, but usually if the bomber can obtain dynamite, he can also get caps. Tape is the most common means of binding sticks of dynamite together, but cloth, wood or paper containers may be used.

Metal that rusts within a few hours of a bombing indicates the presence of oxidizing salts which are found in dynamite. An appearance of spider-web sublimation on the surface of metal at cold temperatures also indicates dynamite.

In a grenade bombing, it will be found that a safety lever will fly off

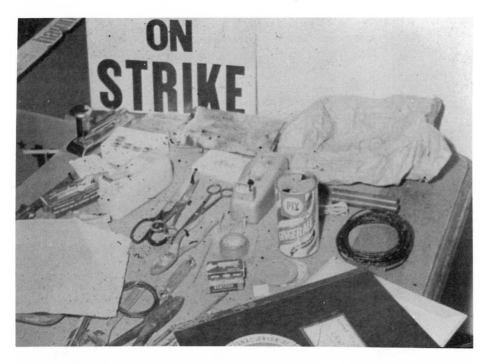

Figure 192. Explosives, tools and materials similar to those in the bomb shown in Figure 157 were found in a suspect's office.

the grenade en route to the target and usually within 25 feet of the thrower (Fig. 193). It should then be unmarked by the explosion. It is possible for a fingerprint or lot number to be found on this lever.

Only in two bombings using time pencils have the safety bands been found at the scene. An examination of the slot in the pencil may reveal a grain of paint to show the color of the band (Figs. 194 and 195).

Victims

The clothing of victims of bombings and amputated parts should be obtained as quickly as possible after a bombing to prevent them from being discarded. Explosive residue and bomb parts may be embedded in a person and only x-rays will disclose it. The chain of custody for these items should be as secure as possible. Since 50 percent of the victims of bombings may be the perpetrators, speed of recovery may be essential. Photographs should be taken of victims to show injuries before they heal. The extent of injuries, the type and location of injuries will show proximity and location of the victim to the explosion.

Figure 193. The author is shown pointing to where the grenade safety lever flew off the grenade between the thrower and the crater.

To protect the victims and to avoid civil responsibility, persons who have been near explosions but show no outward sign of injury should be routinely examined for damage to ears and lungs. Broken eardrums and hearing nerve damage often occurs, and unless a thorough examination is given, the victim may not know about it for years. Similarly, x-rays may show lung tumors of unknown origin at a later date, so victims should have chest x-rays after exposure to an explosion.

Examination of victims of bombings in Ulster disclosed that many of the injuries were due to bursting of liquid-filled portions of the bodies. Blood vessels, digestive systems, kidneys and spleens rupture due to explosion pressures causing faster vibrations in those body parts than in others. Before that time, others had thought that many unmarked bodies had died as the results of vacuum effects of explosions.

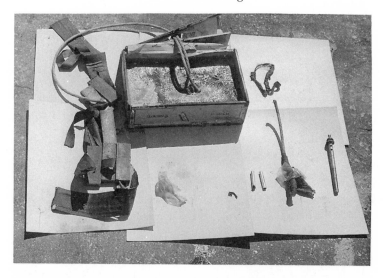

Figure 194. In this bomb, a time pencil and caps were placed inside a prophylactic which was attached to det cord leading to a pentolite cast in a cigar box. Magnets were used to attach the bomb to the ship shown in Figure 195. A telephone number on the box led to the arrest of the group that was responsible. The safety band from the time pencil was found to be still intact inside the prophylactic.

Figure 195. The author removed and deactivated this bomb in the water and finished dismantling it on the dock. This limpit mine had been attached four feet below the waterline of the ship shown in the background.

Vehicles

Figure 196 is a fine example of preservation of bombing evidence involving vehicles. The Dade County Medical Examiner's Office has a garage just for that purpose. Vehicles are transported under wraps to keep possible evidence from falling off while in transit.

Figure 196. A bombed vehicle is shown being lowered from its wrapper on a tow truck. This slide-on tow truck and wrapper helped to prevent any loss of evidence en route to the examination and comparison garage at the medical examiner's office.

In the examination of vehicle bombings it usually facilitates the investigation by obtaining an identical or similar vehicle for comparison of parts. New car dealers are usually cooperative in furnishing duplicate vehicles and mechanics to assist in advice. For court purposes, confiscated vehicles may be obtained for explosive demonstrations. Sophisticated electronics and wiring complicates the examination of bombed modern vehicles.

Ship Bombings

For underwater collection of evidence these procedures have been used in the fifteen ship bombings that the author has investigated. The surface of the water is searched and floating debris is collected before tide, current or wind disperses it further. Shore areas that may have been used by divers or small boats are searched and possible witnesses interviewed by investigators. Police divers will do underwater examination, photography and measurements of the damaged area. A search of the bottom of the body of water by divers may locate heavy fragments just lying on the bottom. Fragments lose velocity in short distances in water.

Bar magnets, as shown in Figure 197, dragged through the water on lines about at a 45-degree angle from a boat will collect most small magnetic particles lying on the bottom of the water. Figure 198 shows a bomb that had been placed below the waterline.

Figure 197. Criminalist Newton Porter is using the bar magnet to drag the bottom of a canal after a boat bombing. The divers should complete their search of the bottom of the water beforehand, as the magnet will tend to disturb it. The bomb mechanism had been placed along the shore, underneath the dock.

After the use of magnets dragged from the surface, divers may then use suction pumps to sift the water bottom, usually mud, sand and silt, in searching for bomb fragments collected in sieves as shown in Figure 199.

A seagoing patch as shown in Figure 200 that was applied by Byrd Marine Salvage will permit the ship to be pumped out and preserve evidence inside the hull of the ship. Figure 201 depicts a Russian ship in dry dock in New Jersey. The author examined and collected evidence inside the hull.

Figure 198. The damage caused by this ship bombing was covered over with a seagoing patch by the Byrd Salvage Company. Notice the zinc plates attached to the ship, which can be mistaken for limpit mines at first glance.

LABORATORY EXAMINATION

The laboratories of the Federal Bureau of Investigation and the Bureau of Alcohol, Tobacco and Firearms can analyze residues of an explosive. The purpose of submission of bombing evidence to the laboratory may be for one or several reasons: identification, analysis and/or comparison of fingerprints, shoe or tire impressions, tool marks, fracture patterns, composition of materials, trace analysis, reconstruction and sources. The examination of explosive cartridges and containers and bombing evidence for fingerprints are improved considerably by expediting the process. The sooner a surface can be examined with cyanoacrylate or ninhydrin, as shown in Figure 202, the better the results. The investigator who collects and preserves the evidence may decide to submit each fragment in a separate container as seen in Figure 203. In court later, it may be impressive to state, for example, that there are over a hundred pieces of evidence that are similar to evidence recovered from the defendant in fabric comparison. On the other hand, it may be simpler to put all similar fragments from the scene in one container because at the laboratory the criminalist may find it easier and less time consuming. The criminalist may find it less trouble collectively to analyze trace

Figure 199. This type of suction pump has been used by divers searching treasure ships which have disintegrated. In searching for evidence, the water is pumped through sieves on the shore at this ship-bombing scene.

nitrates or to reconstruct small fragments for identification. Searching for fracture pattern comparison with evidence from the suspect is facilitated for the criminalist if all similar fragments are submitted together.

In the laboratory chemists may open each container and examine every particle, bit by bit, with a low-power microscope, looking for unexploded explosives and explosive residues. Suspect material is examined under polarizing microscopes to compare crystalline structure with known crystal standards of explosives. X-ray diffraction has been replaced by other more modern instrumentation. The scanning electron microscope can be used for rapid comparison of known standards from previous testing.

Thin-layer chromatography can be performed in any laboratory to identify explosive residue. Vacuum extraction of suspected hydrocarbons from containers of arson evidence can be separated into components by a gas chromatograph. Mass spectrographic analysis may identify the chemicals involved. Wet chemical analysis and infrared spectrophotometry are also used in the laboratory for examination of bombing evidence.

Figure 200. This seagoing patch was applied at sea by the Byrd Salvage Company after this first of a series of ship bombings in the Miami area. The bomb was put on the ship in Miami and it exploded off Key West. After the patch was applied, the ship was repaired in Mobile. Screw hook bolts and cement were applied by divers in this risky operation.

Figure 201. The author was hired by the ship's agent in New Jersey to determine the cause of the explosive damage on this ship which had exploded in Puerto Rico. Evidence was submitted to the FBI for examination and comparison.

Large pieces of debris may be x-rayed to disclose embedded bomb fragments.

Laboratory reports should advise the investigator what materials should be listed on a search warrant of the possible suspect's home, vehicle, house, workshop or test area to connect the suspect with a bombing. If a

Figure 202. Ninhydrin spray is one of the techniques that has helped develop latent finger-prints in bombings. The Brodie magnet lift technique is another new technique utilizing the MacDonald magna brush to lift latent prints developed with magnetic powders. Simply running a magnet over the top of lifting tape makes the magnetic particles adhere to the lifting tape. The lift is better than some of the photographs of a print developed with a magna brush.

Figure 203. Photographs should be taken of evidence before it is submitted to a laboratory. It may be a long time before the evidence is examined by the laboratory and returned.

suspect has a chance to get rid of evidence, an investigator may have to resort to explosive vapor detection by dogs or machines. Explosive smear detection as shown in Figure 204 may help. Vacuum sweepings and the examination of trash containers have proven to be of value. If a suspect is arrested with explosives or bomb parts in his possession, the items should be examined for fingerprints. The fingerprints may be identified with other suspects or the suspect may deny that he knew the material in question was there.

Figure 204. People who collect evidence on explosive incidents should have a close liaison with criminalists who process the evidence. In some cases, it is helpful to have a criminalist come to the scene to assist the evidence technicians to decide what, how and how much evidence they want.

RECONSTRUCTION OF BOMB

Evidence obtained in the manner described may be of great value in determining the origin of the bomb and thereby aid in bringing about the arrest of the perpetrators. The source of the material used in the bomb should be traced to determine manufacturers, distributors and users. With some legwork, it may be found that a particular part may be rare, and the bomber may therefore be identified as a purchaser. One Cuban bought a particular type of relay sold only in Chicago, because the relay was impervious to shock. Teaspoon-size fragments of dynamite can be analyzed to find the manufacturer free of charge by the DuPont Company, since the companies analyze competitors' products constantly (Fig. 205).

Figure 205. A stick of dynamite with a piece of cotton rope was found wrapped in newspaper outside the Orange Bowl Stadium the day President Kennedy greeted the returned Bay of Pigs prisoners at the stadium. The dynamite was not in its original container. The DuPont Company conducted an analysis which showed that it was not manufactured in the United States.

Reconstruction of a bomb can lead to valuable clues for the bomb technician as he puts it together with exactly the same type of parts in exactly the same way as the bomber did as shown in Figure 206. This may reveal evidence such as possible tool impressions or fingerprints as shown in Figure 207. The *modus operandi* of fabrication of a bomb and the method of delivery have become known as the signature of a bomber. Signature may also refer to the effects of a bomb. Bombers tend to repeat their work. If a method or material works, they may use it again. Staking out sources of material may be worthwhile.

Figure 206. The author and FBI Agent Bob Mills are shown collecting evidence that was embedded in a fence at a bombing scene. The perpetrator had returned to the scene, dismantled it and then placed it under another car when he found out later that he had placed the bomb under the wrong car. The victim lost both legs in this cocaine war bombing.

Visual aids for teaching purposes are just as valuable in court testimony in illustrating how dangerous bombs are even when dummy materials are used. Standing in front of the jury and reconstructing a dummy bomb and then showing how it works really lets a jury decide to convict a defendant. In one bombing, the author obtained the dummy materials which were given to the bomber to reconstruct in the courtroom. He testified against the drug dealers who had hired him. When he first saw the reconstructed bomb, he said, "That's exactly how I made it."

After a bomber is convicted, the investigator should contact the parole officer who may be in charge of the pre-sentence investigation. The investigator may disclose information about all previous investigations and possible related cases where the subject may have been involved.

Figure 207. The suspect in this bombing of a locker at the Miami International Airport was convicted due to a latent fingerprint lift from the handle of the locker by these three bomb technicians.

The investigator should also contact the prosecutor and testify to this information and advise the court whether he believes the subject should receive the maximum sentence.

Later, the investigator should talk with the subject in prison to attempt to develop him as an informant. In any attempts at parole, the investigator may wish to advise the parole board whether the subject should remain in prison.

Explosive evidence should be retained as long as possible. Explosives should not be destroyed in a possible criminal case unless the judge orders it. A defense attorney may wish for his expert to examine all or part of the explosives.

Bomb evidence should be retained forever for two reasons. First, the defendant may obtain a new trial years later and similar bombs of the same *modus operandi* have been found in cases as much as sixteen years later.

EXPLOSIVE EVIDENCE CHECKLIST PROCEDURE

The following steps are a guide and will vary with the individual situation.

Upon Arrival

1. Contact officer or complainant for information on explosion.
2. Set up barriers beyond where most distant debris is found.

Gas Explosion

1. Determine if any gas tanks or gas lines are present.
2. Determine if anyone smelled gas before explosion.
3. Determine if gas is still leaking.
4. Turn off gas lines.
5. Request gas company to cut off gas lines.
6. Put out fires.
7. Dissipate fumes by ventilation or water.
8. Take sample of escaped gas where smell is strongest.
9. Trace gas lines to open or broken line.
10. Determine position of all valves.
11. Determine all possible sources of ignition.

Arson Explosion

1. Determine hot spot.
2. Look for unburned accelerant.
3. Smell for accelerants around hot spots.
4. Find steam craters on concrete floors.
5. Look for accelerant cans or containers.
6. Search for incendiary-delay devices.
7. Examine entrance doors and windows, whether they are locked or unlocked, or whether the bomber forced entry.

Bombing

1. Search area for other bombs.
2. Find center (crater or seat) of explosion.
3. Find most distant fragments from center of explosion.
4. Set up search teams to check perimeters for evidence.
5. Have bomb technician search obvious remote areas.
6. Take photographs of overall scene.
7. Take photographs of fragments in relation to background.
8. Take ruled photograph of crater showing depth and width.
9. Measure depth by stretching a line from edges of crater and measuring vertically from line to bottom.

10. Smell crater, wood or cloth to determine sweet or acrid odor and amount of odor.
11. Search crater for fragments of bomb.
12. Search area for fragments of bomb.
13. Sweep and shovel small debris into clean garbage cans and boxes.
14. Search large debris for holes and probe holes for fragments of bomb.
15. Take measurements for scaled floor plan of area.
16. If outside, measure distance to closest building.
17. Measure distance to closest person and witness.
18. Describe damage in notes.
19. Measure to most distant point of damage.
20. Examine entrance doors and windows, whether locked, unlocked or forced entry.
21. Sift all debris at office through ½-inch, ¼-inch and ⅛-inch screens respectively, searching for unknown fragments.
22. Take scaled photograph of all fragments of bomb.
23. Submit fragments of bomb and soot and residue on fragments to ATF or FBI Laboratory for analysis of type of explosive.
24. Call ATF or FBI Laboratory before unexploded explosive is submitted for analysis.

Question Witnesses

1. Did you see the bomber(s)?
2. What was bomber's action before, during and after explosion?
3. What was bomber's direction to and from scene?
4. Do you know the name or identity of the bomber?
5. Was there fire, smoke or sound before explosion?
6. What was the color and size of fireball?
7. What was the color of smoke?
8. What was the type of sound; i.e. sharp, crack, boom, muffled, or repeated?
9. What was the position of witness from explosion?

Chapter 11

PRINCIPLES OF BOMB PROTECTION

A nyone who is concerned with the protection of people or property from bombs is knowingly, or unknowingly, following one or more of the following principles of bomb protection. This chapter is a checklist or guideline to permit full use of the principles for maximum benefit of bomb safety.

INTELLIGENCE

The first line of defense is intelligence information. There is absolutely no substitute for advance information as to who, when, where, what, how and why a target may be bombed. Intelligence information has been defined simply as just knowing what is going on. An intelligence operation is similar to a criminal investigation, except that information is gathered in many instances before a criminal act takes place in an effort to prevent the act from occurring or to minimize its effects.

The four parts of a criminal investigation—interview, gathering evidence, surveillance and use of records—all apply to intelligence work. Information is gathered and the problem is analyzed so decisions can be made as to what protective measures should be taken. Without information, lives, property, time and other resources may be wasted.

As in good investigations, all sources of information are used: informants, other agencies, statistics, police intelligence, similar and local businesses, residents, employees, professional organizations, news media, local affairs, security and bomb disposal associations.

Infiltration of possible terrorist bombing groups may be made through their ancillary supporters or radical activists. Associates of terrorists are involved in the movement of personnel and equipment for terrorists. These supporters provide security, publicity, supplies, safe houses, communications, recruitment, lawyers, negotiations, money and political contacts. Support groups, sympathizers or political activists may knowingly or unknowingly select and surveil targets for bombers.

Analysis

Interpretation of all known facts and unconfirmed information are used in developing the level of threat assessment. The threat level fluctuates and the amount of preparation varies with it.

As in other forms of security, physical strengths and weaknesses are evaluated concerning protection of people or property from bombs. One may think as a bomber and do a target analysis. How critical is the target? How accessible is it? How quickly can the target be replaced or recuperate? What will be the inconvenience to the target? What is the target's value and purpose? What is the risk to the bombers? What are the chances of being apprehended or killed? What will be the resultant publicity? Whoever is involved in bomb protection should assess the target, possible bombers and bombs.

Analysis of who would possibly wish to bomb a target also requires information concerning bombers. Various motives and purposes of various individuals and groups who may wish to bomb a target may be evaluated. Past, current and future events may initiate a possible bomber. Common motives for bombings are political, revenge, profit, religious and labor disputes.

Evaluation of intelligence information is an awesome responsibility. Dissemination of intelligence information is another difficult decision. Whether to publish openly to everyone in a public awareness program or to advise only a select group who are on a need-to-know basis may be critical.

How a recipient of intelligence information reacts in utilizing the principles of bomb protection may be crucial to those involved.

DISTANCE

The main form of protection from bombs is distance. The best protection from bombs is to stay away from them. Distance may be important in several different ways: from the effects of heat, pressure fragmentation and vacuum. Pressure at the center of a bomb explosion may be as high as one million pounds per square inch. Heat at the center of an explosion may reach 9,000° F. Fragmentation near the center of an explosion may travel faster than a bullet. The vacuum effect may break windows at long distances from the center of an explosion. The tremendous pressure at the center of an explosion falls off in inverse square proportions.

Chances of being hit by fragmentation also fall off rapidly with short increases in distance. For instance, a person one foot away from the explosion of a fragmentation hand grenade has a 100 percent chance of being struck by a fragment. At three feet the chances of being struck by a fragment are one out of nine, and at nine feet away the chances are one out of twenty-five of being hit. Fireballs only last a split second and are usually very small. The main injuries to people from vacuum effect is caused by falling glass. Distance is the best form of protection from bombs.

Another important consideration of distance is the length which a bomb or bomber must travel to arrive at a target. By increasing this dimension the bomber and the type of bomb may be limited. The delivery method of being placed, dropped, thrown or projected can be curtailed in bomb protection preparations. Small bombs may be easier for a bomber to carry concealed to his target and large bombs may be blocked by limited access.

Distance is a factor in how much area has to be protected from a bomber. The smaller the area, the less time it takes to search and the fewer personnel are necessary.

The distance that a person or object is traveling may lengthen the time necessary to protect that target and increase its vulnerability.

The main reason distance is important is to know which direction to go in order to stay away from bombs.

BARRIERS

At one time, protection from bombs was understood to be of two types: distance and barriers. Many bomb specialists still know only these two methods.

Two axioms about barriers are essential to remember when preparing bomb protection. Barriers create distance. Barriers shorten distance. With barriers one is able to keep potential bombers and bombs from getting near a target. A dirt berm may lessen the distance one has to be from the effects of a bomb.

The author has divided barriers into three types: observation, prevention and attenuation. Barriers may serve one, two or all three functions. Observation barriers are designed to shield the target from possible or known bomber(s). A barrier may block visibility so most people do not know it is a possible target, what it is or what its function is.

Natural barriers like earth are usually the simplest, most economical and effective means of shielding from the ground or from the air. Caves, tunnels and mines may be supplemented with berms, parapets and ramparts. Solid walls like the Berlin Wall, as shown in Figure 208, used to block some observation as well as access. The Iron Curtain, as shown in Figure 209, prevented access. This three-meter high steel screen was backed up by three meters of mine fields, a patrol road, observation towers, cleared fields, radar, binoculars, sound detectors and night-vision enhancement. Cost is a big factor in determining the type and extent of barriers.

Figure 208. The author took this photograph of the Berlin Wall being dismantled at the conclusion of the Cold War.

Preventive barriers are those which deter bombers from getting to a target. Fences, guards, checkpoints, ditches, lights, alarms, explosive mines and other such security measures are preventive barriers.

Technical or bomb effect attenuation barriers are specifically designed to deflect, reflect, absorb or dissipate the pressure, heat, fragmentation and vacuum effects of a bomb explosion. Attenuation or mitigation mean to lessen force, strength or severity effects which may cause casualties or damage. Each type of barrier would be examined in depth and analyzed to determine if the circumstances merit its use.

Figure 209. The enormous financial cost of the Iron Curtain helped to defeat it. The cost of each bomb protection principle is of prime consideration and must be justified with statistics in budgeting.

The best people who are used for advice on the subject of barriers are bomb disposal technicians or explosive ordnance disposal personnel. When police chiefs, commanding officers, chief executive officers, contractors and architects become concerned with trying to improve bomb resistance of new or existing structures, they will rely on the bomb squad or EOD for information.

BOMBCAD™ is a computerized program to estimate bomb damage vulnerability of structures. This computerized concept is used in designing new buildings to help minimize intrusion of bombs and bomb effects. Walls, floors and roofs are all barriers. Doors, windows, and air conditioning access not only provide easier introduction of bombs but also are weak points against bomb effects. Windows may be reinforced with grenade screens to keep out thrown bombs or with clear, heavy polyester film containing nylon monofilaments with acrylic adhesive. The film may prevent intrusion of bombs as well as bomb effects.

HUMAN RESOURCES

One of the main methods of protection from bombs is the proper utilization of people. The best way to dispose of bombs is to get someone else to do it for you. There are a lot of functions that different people can do in bomb protection. The different classes of human resources are management, bomb disposal technicians, victims, government, employees, armed forces, police and fire personnel.

Command

Bomb disposal is a one-man job. Bomb protection involves the cooperation and combined effort of many different people. Management or command personnel have the overall responsibility of insuring that the principles of bomb protection are applied. Command may be anyone who has, takes or is given the responsibility for the safety of people or property from bombs. To do the job correctly he or she assesses the bomb threat level. The best quality personnel are obtained and given the best training and equipment.

Management should set up a table of organization and establish standard operating procedures. Financing must be arranged for set programs. Purposes and goals are developed, understood and performed. Command insures internal and external communications. Bomb protection covers a lot more functions than drawing up a bomb-scare plan.

Bomb Disposal Technicians

A civilian bomb squad or a military explosive ordnance disposal unit is an important human resource in bomb protection planning. In order to properly prepare, management must find out who they are and what their availability is. Management may have to decide whether to have their own bomb squad or to borrow the nearest bomb squad's services. Two problems to be decided are jurisdiction and financial responsibility.

Communications must be established with existing bomb squads who will provide advice on bomb protection planning. Management or command should know if a bomb squad will respond under what circumstances. Notification and response time may be critical. Any information concerning a bomb squad's responsibilities and liabilities should be in writing. Therefore, in emergencies no delay will be involved.

If command decides to have their own bomb squad, then command must be prepared to finance it properly for the safety of all concerned. Command must provide equipment, training, a proper table of organization and standard operating procedures. It is a further function of management to follow up to insure that the safest methods of bomb disposal are being used by the members of the bomb squad.

Victims, Family and Friends

Most of the time it is helpful to obtain as much help as possible in bomb protection. This may be done with public awareness programs in some cases or through personal contact with possible victims, their relatives or friends. Establishing a rapport with victims may lead to their cooperation in efforts to protect their lives and property. Management may have to advise victims of the level of the threat and how self-help can make the job of protection safer and easier. Motivation is established through two-way open communications. Cooperation, information, and public support in intelligence, investigations, alertness and searching may all be beneficial to all concerned.

Management should convince possible victims, relatives and friends that their cooperation is their best hope for protection. Training of victims to be wary of suspicious objects, how to avoid them or report them are good public awareness programs.

Government

One of the reasons for government to exist is to protect its citizens. Government, whether it is local, state or federal, should plan for bomb protection of its citizens. If a particular government does not have a bomb squad, then that particular government in question should have arrangements with another government agency from whom it can request bomb disposal service. The government should have a bomb protection plan to instruct its citizens in proper training and safety from bomb threats and scares. If they do not have such a training policy, then it should have some other governmental agency or private source to instruct its citizens in proper training and safety from bomb threats and scares.

Government has the financial responsibility of providing for all of the above functions for the safety of its citizens and their property. If government decides it does not have the finances to do so, then it should have arrangements in writing with other governmental agencies to do so.

The preamble of the American Constitution states that among other purposes, the United States was formed to establish justice, insure domestic tranquility, provide for the common defense and promote the general welfare. If the existing laws of a community do not provide for proper protection by not covering the use of explosives, for example, then new legislation should be provided.

Employees

In the protection of any business from bombs, employees become heavily involved. Employees are advised of the level of bomb threats. Employees are placed on the alert to avoid intrusion of bombs into their area. Employees are taught the necessity of good housekeeping and security measures. Search plan training should be given to all employees. Practice bomb drills help boost employee morale and cooperation.

Armed Forces

Civilians may have to rely on the explosive ordnance disposal teams of the United States Armed Forces for bomb disposal. The armed forces depend on their own personnel for security measures against terrorist and extremist bombings. Military personnel are trained in prevention of terrorist attacks which are undeclared and unconventional war.

Bombings and other attacks may take place at the least expected times and at any target that may represent the United States. On-duty and off-duty personnel may be attacked on or off military installations. Personnel are trained in identification through recognition of improvised explosive devices and delivery methods.

Members of the armed forces who are on foreign assignments should especially know the bomb threat level of their assignment and keep abreast of other bombings, dissidents and of other aspects of intelligence information on a need-to-know basis. Military personnel overseas should provide protective barriers against the delivery of bombs by every possible method. All suspicious incidents should be reported. Personnel should be alert for suspect items and be aware that explosive ordnance disposal people are charged with the responsibility of the disposition of all unknown suspicious improvised explosive devices.

Police

In most parts of the United States, bomb and explosive problems become a matter for the police to handle. The duties of bomb disposal, bomb protection, investigation and intelligence information may be in separate sections of a police department. Besides establishing a table of organization for these functions, the police must establish communications for these functions. It is the duty of police to also secure funding for this and provide citizens' awareness programs including model bomb search procedures.

Police departments have to protect their own citizens and their own personnel and property from possible bombings.

Fire Departments

Fire departments should maintain relations with police for arson and explosion investigations. In many jurisdictions fire personnel are also rescue personnel. Rescue personnel may be especially trained in handling victims of explosions. Fire and rescue personnel may stand by at scenes of recovered explosives, bomb disposal activities, bombings and explosions.

Fire personnel may be trained in gas fires and preservation of burning explosives scenes.

During the last decade, the problem of hazardous material has become more and more the province of fire departments. Hazardous Materials Teams or HAZMAT equipment and training is an expensive and dangerous specialty. The trend has been for bomb squads to dispose of some fuels and oxidizers, while HAZMAT takes care of other dangerous chemicals that will not explode.

DETECTION

Bomb detection is one of the basic principles of bomb protection. Detection is divided into two categories: (1) prevention of bombs from arriving at the target you wish to protect and (2) the discovery of bombs that have already arrived at the target. There are three factors that determine if a bomb can be detected: (1) personnel and equipment, (2) the bomb and the bomber, and (3) the target itself.

Personnel and Equipment

Personnel and equipment are forms of barriers which may be overt or covert. Personnel and equipment may act as deterrents to bombers, but they may also be an indication of a possible target and act as a challenge to possible bombers. The number of people and their knowledge are important. Proper motivation of personnel is a function of management by keeping their bomb detection personnel advised of intelligence information on a need-to-know basis.

The five senses of sight, sound, smell, touch and taste plus deductive reasoning may be enhanced with many different types of equipment. Visual acuity is most commonly aided with lights and eyeglasses. Magnification is further assisted with telescopes, binoculars and hand lens. X-ray, infrared and ultraviolet lighting are becoming more commonplace and should be considered when trying to develop or improve a bomb protection plan. Mirrors, television cameras, video recorders, telephoto lens and still cameras may be desirable, depending upon the individual circumstances and finances.

Hearing may be improved by microphones to pick up sound from suspect items, both by contact or from distances. Recording conversations is common intelligence-gathering operations regarding bomb protection. Animals are used to detect sounds of possible intruder(s) who may try to bring bombs into a protected area.

The sense of smell has become an important means of explosive detection in the last quarter of the century. Dogs are the primary means, but electronic detection of explosive odors assists our own sense of smell. The best form of protection is to utilize all three. Continuous research and development projects supplemented by federal funding hopefully will make machine detection of explosive odors more reliable.

Touch sensitivity is used in the hand searching of luggage for detecting hardness and weight of objects. Mine clearing involves a real sense of touch. Searchers of buildings and vehicles during bomb scares often rely on their sense of touch. Bomb disposal technicians use their sense of touch in the use of robots, remote shields and hands-on dismantling of bombs.

The sense of taste is used rarely and with caution to test a suspected explosive. This method of detection is not recommended.

Bomb and Explosive Detection Factors

If a bomb is to be detected, the personnel who are to be charged with that responsibility should be able to recognize certain characteristics of explosives and bombs. Identification through recognition of explosive or bomb containers and initiation systems depends on the knowledge and training of the individual bomb searchers. Simple nomenclature terminology training of searching personnel may help detect a bomb.

Target

The following conditions of a target may decide if particular types of bombs can reach the target without detection or be found once any bombs are at a target. The size of the area to be protected or searched is a prime consideration. This may be increased or diminished, depending on whether it is found to be helpful or harmful to the people responsible for protection. Atmospheric conditions of humidity, temperature, pressure and visibility all may affect detection efforts. Wind and water currents, time and contaminants sometimes will help or hinder the project. The age of the explosive and its time at the target may affect the condition of the explosive. Vapors may accumulate or dissipate with time and atmospheric conditions. Contaminating vapors, brush, trash and large quantities of material may all be factors that determine whether a successful search is conducted.

MOTION, DECOYS AND DIVERSIONS

A moving target is more difficult to hit. A moving target may also be more difficult to detect or see. On the other hand, motion may attract attention and therefore the motion of a decoy may become a diversion to draw attention away from a protected target.

Motion may be used to create distance between a bomb and target by moving the target out of the sight and hearing of a possible bomber. An axiom of bomb protection regarding motion is, "Move the people away from a bomb. Do not move a bomb away from the people." Remember that some bombs will explode if they are moved. Save lives first. Save property second.

When bombing a target, whether it be a person or property, a bomber must place, drop, throw or project a bomb. Moving the target and/or using decoys or diversions may spoil a bomber's aim. Target surveillance by a bomber may be disrupted by diversions which may ruin his opportunity. False information, evasive routes and changed schedules have been practiced by people who thought they were objects of possible bombers.

Harassing suspicious persons may not permit them time to prepare for bombings. The motion of a bomber makes him noticeable. Anti-motion alarms can be used against bombers to help prevent their intrusion into an area.

Bomb disposal technicians are constantly aware that controlling motion may be essential in the dismantling of bombs. Possible victims of bombs should be cognizant that certain motions may prevent a bomb from exploding: lack of speed, different direction or not enough distance covered by a movement.

KNOWLEDGE AND MOTIVATION

Knowledge of bomb protection is obtained through training, study, testing and experience. Management or command should have that knowledge to properly prepare a bomb protection program. If command does not have sufficient knowledge of each phase of bomb protection, then command must rely upon the advice of personnel under his management or from other groups. It is up to management to determine if more knowledge or training is necessary for all the people involved. Finances of training, equipment and personnel time are all cost factors to be determined.

Safety is the prime consideration in any bomb protection preparations. Without a proper knowledge of bombs and bombers, command must rely on police and bomb squads for information. Bomb squad and security personnel may find that they need additional communication skills, i.e. speaking and writing. Unless one is able to express one's needs and recommendations properly, disasters may occur. All too often, uninformed· victims or authorities will depend upon their own limited knowledge of bomb protection or rely upon protection from inexperienced bomb personnel who have inadequate knowledge themselves.

Personnel in each function owe it to their interest in their own safety to learn as much about their individual jobs in bomb protection. If a person is a victim, he or she has to be motivated to cooperate, follow advice, practice security and be alert for possible dangerous bombs.

Security personnel have to be motivated to be aware of all applicable intelligence information and to be alert at all times. Police and security organizations provide information and training that are not available through regular chain of command at places of employment.

Bomb disposal technicians really have a need to know in many different areas. They require at least eight to sixteen hours of training per month with equipment. Bomb disposal technicians also need time to maintain equipment and to study. These hours of study, maintenance, practice and refresher training must be budgeted by management.

Nowadays, because of the wealth of material available, there is little excuse of anyone in bomb disposal not to be well informed on the subject. The author realized early that his life depended upon his knowledge. In a jurisdiction where there are a lot of bombs, a technician will find it worth spending his own time and money to learn as much as possible of the many phases of bomb disposal work. A bomb disposal technician's increased knowledge enables him to make the best judgment for the welfare of those whom he is duty-bound to protect.

ELIMINATION OF SOURCES OF BOMB MATERIALS

There are many different ways of stopping a possible bomber or bomb. Elimination of his sources of explosives and bomb-making materials is a primary principle of bomb protection. An offensive move can be made by investigating his resources. Determining where he gets his money is one of the first steps in attacking a bomber. If he has a job or is given money by sympathizers, the problem is changing the sympathizers' rationale. If a bomber or his associates do robberies or other crimes to finance bombing activities, then that is another act that can be attacked and possibly stopped.

Explosives, detonators, initiating systems and containers are all part of bombs that may be traced to their sources. It may not be sufficient to just control explosives but also to control materials that are used to make explosives, i.e. fuels and fertilizers. Regulations and laws may have to be devised and passed. Salaries and positions may have to be allocated to prevent possible materials to be used for bombs.

INTERDICTION

Bombs and/or bombers can be prevented from reaching their targets through aggressive tactics. The most peaceful means are through negotiations.

Changing the Rationale of Bombers

Prevention of a bombing is a lot easier than dismantling bombs or trying to arrest and convict a bomber. It is difficult to measure in statistics how many bombs have been prevented through the changing of possible bombers' thinking. This may start with early childhood.

The education of children at home, school and religious centers in non-violent settlement of disputes may eventually produce adults who do not think of using bombings or violence to gain their goals. Peace education teaches people to resolve conflicts within themselves, among people, groups and nations. These idealistic utopean methods of Jesus Christ and Mahatma Gandhi are being tried in character education public school programs. Hopefully, teaching children right from wrong may prevent some bombings in the future.

Unfortunately, various peace movements have been originated or infiltrated by extremists who are too impatient to bring about change by peaceful methods and consequently do bombings under the guise of peace. The violent methods of some peace movements are diametrically opposed to non-violent settlement of disputes.

Contacts with bombers, whether they are individuals or members of groups, may be made through public awareness programs, the news media, informants or support groups. Rapport and negotiations may be conducted with possible bombers even though their identify may not be known. Trying to determine bombers' motives may result in removal of the reasons for bombing. Political compromises or financial settlements may prevent the possibility of future bloodshed or disturbances and result in mutual cooperation.

The psychological profiling of bombers in the past by the United States Department of Justice leads to the identity of present bombers and also helps in dialogues with them. George Metesky, the original Mad Bomber of New York City, was a prime example of a perpetrator explaining why he performed his bombings. Logic can be used to convince a bomber, his relatives or friends to stop his crimes or surrender to authorities.

Financial rewards or the citing of punishment for bombing or accessories to the act may change a bomber or his friends into informants. Rewards, fear, revenge and conscience regarding patriotism or a sense of duty are all reasons that can be used in dealing with bombers.

Removing the Cause

As the Irish Republican Army says, "It's all for the cause," no matter if they kill innocent women and children or some of their own people. If you can determine what the cause is and what may motivate someone or some group to bomb, you may help to prevent future occurrences of bombings by removing the cause to bomb. However, if any concessions are given, it may only serve to further inspire the cause. Often, concessions are regarded by bombers as weaknesses. Bombers respect strength and force. Vacillation or equivocation from administration may encourage more bombings. The best plan may be to make change and by drawing attention to it.

The most optimistic approach is to not give anyone a reason to bomb in the first place. The reason or purpose to bomb may be because of labor disputes, religious disputes, political disputes, or revenge for profit. Individuals, activists or extremists may be goaded into bombing due to frustrations in their efforts to bring about change through peaceful means. People who may become targets because of some act should think through the consequences of their action. Antagonizing someone may psychologically force them into drastic acts of retaliation or intimidation.

When the Vietnamese War was over, the cause of some bombers was lost. A number of Americans were trained by the Cuban military to be revolutionists in the United States during the time. They still have the knowledge and may emerge when a situation is supplied.

When certain politicians are voted out of office, prospective bombers may be satisfied that their cause is no longer necessary. Changes in the policy of a business may prevent strikes and acts of violence.

Appointments, events and meetings that may be possible targets can be cancelled or postponed or the location changed to remove the cause of bombers. If, upon analysis of a problem, it is found that it is a lot easier and safer to remove a cause for bombers and the loss of pride or esteem is negligible, the cause should be withdrawn. One should not stand on pride when dealing with bomb protection. It may be a lot safer to remove reasons for bombers to bomb.

Isolation of Bombers

There are several different methods used by government or law enforcement to separate a bomber from targets: temptation, supplies and support, public exposure, exile or deportation, misinformation, imprisonment, execution, probation, parole and surveillance.

Public awareness programs may isolate a bomber or bombers from society by exposure of their names, causes, addresses and employment. Through this method, bombers may become outcasts of society through ridicule and public condemnation. Exposure of supporters and how money is being spent for bombs and weapons to create orphans and widows instead of worthy causes may isolate bombers from further fund raising and political support. Insufficient evidence for an arrest or conviction does not prevent exposure through news media or grand jury investigations. On the contrary, it may provide bombers with publicity they may be seeking.

Exile or deportation of suspects may be a method that can be applied if insufficient evidence for a conviction exists. Some bomb group leaders will control, supply or teach from abroad.

Misinformation to suspects that they are about to be arrested may cause them to leave a jurisdiction and become probation violators or to leave potential targets in an area that is to be protected from bombs. Misinformation that a suspected bomber is an informant may isolate him from his cohorts.

Imprisonment of a bomber or a group of bombers may be a deterrent to other bombers or potential bombers. But then again, it may cause the arrested person to become a martyr or rallying cry for others to bomb. Several examples of both results have been found in the Miami area. Imprisonment separates bombers from targets, and while in prison they may be developed into informants or be rehabilitated through rationalization.

While in jail, bombers may teach others and after they are released they may again do bombings. The only sure cure for bombers is execution. It is important to keep tabs on bombers in jail to prevent their early release on probation or parole. Upon their release, it is important to keep track of their whereabouts and activities.

Force

A show of force may be a sufficient deterrent to possible bombers. In order to prevent a bomb or bombers from reaching or initiating a bomb at a target, one may have to use weapons as a last resort.

There are many considerations in making decisions on weaponry regarding the type of bomb(s) that may be used, the bomber(s), the target(s) and manpower. Finances, policy and laws may restrict a choice of weapons and how they are used.

An inspection of the target area may give some insight as to the size of bombs, initiation systems, number and delivery methods of possible bombers. Intelligence information may be analyzed as to what to expect from possible enemies as to their motive, determination, objective and suicidal tendencies. Their approach may be surreptious and slow or open and sudden. Bombers may be carrying and using firearms, also.

Open fields of fire or obstacles may help decide on the type of force that can be used to stop bombs or bombers. Innocent people in the area may change policy on the type of weapons or when they can be used to stop bombers or bombs before they get in proximity of a target. All security personnel should know exactly under what condition to carry their weapons and concise and clearly understood instructions as to when weapons can be used.

Human bombs have been used in robbery attempts, assassinations and extortions. Claiming to have a bomb in one's possession is a felony in most jurisdictions. When confronted by a person who claims to have a bomb in his possession, the safest procedure is to create distance between the suspect bomber and the defender, have the defender take cover, make sure the area is clear of innocent people and shoot the perpetrator at the base of the skull. In that manner, the medulla oblongata is no longer able to transmit commands to the body to initiate the bomb. But if the bomb has a deadman's switch, the bomb will explode unless the bomber is alive to hold it open. Trying to forceably remove a bomb from the possession of anyone carrying a bomb or trying to render it safe while fighting him may cause more death and injury to innocent persons than remotely shooting the perpetrator.

INDEX